ARE YOU SURE THIS IS MINE?

A Search for God and Truth

Judy Gill Milford

THE THOMAS MORE PRESS
Chicago, Illinois

Copyright © 1990 by Judy Gill Milford. All rights reserved. Printed in the United States of America. No part of this publication may be reproduced, stored in a retrieval system, or transmitted, in any form or by any means, electronic, mechanical, photocopying, recording, or otherwise, without the written permission of the publisher, The Thomas More Association, 205 W. Monroe St., Chicago, Illinois 60606.

ISBN 0-88347-261-9

Are You Sure This is Mine? is the winner of the 1989 nonfiction book contest for previously unpublished authors sponsored by the Thomas More Press and Father Andrew Greeley. Judy Gill Milford, of Paducah, Kentucky, a poet and writer, is married and the mother of four children.

Part One

Cool Hand Luke and Me

I

Jesus Christ is the same today as he was yesterday and as he will be forever. Do not let yourselves be led astray by all sorts of strange doctrines. . . .
(Hebrews 13:8)

THE newsmen and newspaper talk about Russians wanting power and bombs that could end the world. I lie in bed at night trying to imagine the end of everything. It makes me sick inside. People should know better than to do that to each other. People are building fallout shelters to go into if something like that happens. I don't like to think about it. I don't like to think about a lot of things that go on in the world. On weekends if I stay up late enough watching old movies on TV, I'm so tired when I go to bed that I don't have to lie in the dark and think about bombs and war, killing and death. I don't feel so good watching the news. I don't really like comedy shows, but at least when they are on I don't have to think about the world ending.

* * * *

Judy Gill Milford

I don't know what I'm going to do when I get out of school. If history wasn't so boring and if I could remember all those dates, I would be an archeologist. It would be exciting to dig in the earth and solve mysteries of hundreds and thousands of years ago.

* * * *

I really like people. I think I would like to study psychology in college, but I'm scared to. As a psychologist, I would have to make all the right decisions for people and sometimes I make mistakes. It would be easier for me to decide what I'm going to do if there weren't so many things that I like to do.

* * * *

Nancy, Jean and I went to Cairo tonight. Nancy hoped she would see a boy over there named Robby. She said he is real nice and she would probably like him if he just wasn't Catholic. I don't know very much about Catholics except that Mama knew some when she lived in New Jersey and Pennsylvania. She knew a Catholic girl who lost her watch. She prayed a prayer "Hail Mary" over and over to Mary the mother of Jesus to help her find her watch. I don't know if she ever found it. We only have Methodist, Baptist and Christian churches in Wickliffe and none of them pray to anybody else but God and Jesus.

Mama says it's better not to date a Catholic boy because you never know who you may fall in love

Are You Sure This Is Mine?

with and marry. She said people have to work at having good marriages and being different religions gives you just one more thing that has to be worked out. I guess she is probably right.

* * * *

We have to write a lot of essays and other papers for college prep English. I hate writing assignments. When I try to think of something to write, my mind goes blank. All the papers I get back from the teacher have things written all over them—suggestions for making my writing better. I can't seem to write anything that she likes.

Literature has always been one of my favorite subjects, but I'm not any good at it either. When we read something and tell what it means, I never get the interpretation right. The teacher always tells us what the writer meant, and it is never the same as what I thought.

* * * *

I am going to Lambuth College in the fall. With the National Methodist Scholarship, the National Student Defense Loan and the workshop, I can make it. I still don't know what I will study, but they say you don't have to know right away.

* * * *

Judy Gill Milford

I read the Bible and try to understand it but a lot of it is boring and doesn't make sense. Parts of it are interesting, but I don't understand those parts either. Men laying with women not their wives—holy men. But then we are not supposed to do it until we are married. If it was all right for them to do all the wild things they did, I don't understand why it is wrong for us.

* * * *

My roommate is Marilyn Yates from Kenton, Tennessee. She and I are a lot different but we get along real well. The only thing I don't like about her is that she smokes. I don't really care what she does, but I wish all my clothes didn't smell like smoke.

* * * *

I agree with everybody when they say something. I don't want to make anybody mad or hurt their feelings so I go along with whatever they say. Marilyn called somebody two-faced today for doing that very same thing. I was so surprised. I never wanted to be two-faced; I just wanted people to like me. I didn't want to make anyone mad. I'm going to have to think about that.

* * * *

Are You Sure This Is Mine?

I thought Marilyn and I were such good friends. Tonight, with some other girls, we were watching a movie where Negroes were mistreated and they all called me "nigger lover" because I took up for the Negroes. I didn't know what to say, I was so surprised. I always thought you were supposed to accept a person for what he was instead of judging because of skin color or religion or something like that. I never expected to be judged for not judging. There are a lot of things I don't understand.

* * * *

I am going with the nicest boy. We went almost all year without finding each other. He is a ministerial student and he says he loves me. It would be neat to be a minister's wife. That would probably be a good thing for me to be.

* * * *

During chapel today the speaker announced scholarship winners from last year. Dutch asked me why I never told him about mine. I didn't tell him it was because he was having trouble with his grades and I didn't want to make him feel bad. Besides I feel funny about the scholarship anyway. I should be doing something great for the Methodist Church since they had confidence in me and I am just a nothing. If

Judy Gill Milford

they had known they would have surely given it to someone more deserving.

* * * *

Looking back on my relationship with Dutch, I realize it was not founded on truth. I was so eager to make him feel good about himself that I never let him know anything about me. He never really knew who I was. I don't even know if I know.

* * * *

Some of my friends took some Negro students from Lane College with them to church Sunday. If I had not been afraid of getting in trouble, I would have gone with them. Some of the trustees of our school are mad. I didn't know the Civil War was still being fought until I came down here to school. It can't be wrong for all people to go to church together. God made us all.

* * * *

I had to take New and Old Testament classes here at school, but I don't feel very religious. The religion professors don't seem to believe the same things I was taught when I was a little girl. Science makes religion almost impossible to believe. I would never tell

Are You Sure This Is Mine?

anyone this, but I don't even know if I believe in God. I want to, but how can I? I don't know what to believe.

* * * *

On the way to the cafeteria from class, someone told me that President Kennedy had been shot. At first everyone thought it was a sick joke, but it has happened. We are holding prayer vigils in the chapel. One of the boys in English class said he was glad it happened. How can anyone be that cruel? Marilyn and I went for a long walk in the rain to talk about what has happened. The weather has changed to reflect the mood of the nation. It is dark, cold and so windy that our umbrellas were blown inside out. I called Mama on the phone just to hear her voice. I needed to know that some things are still the same.

* * * *

In the mail today was the greatest surprise—a letter from a boy I met at the Methodist Student Movement Conference at Lake Junaluska. He was so cute and popular with everybody at the conference that I never expected to hear from him. He asked me if I had read a book called *The Prophet* by Kahlil Gibran. I'm going to look for it at the library. He also invited me to go to homecoming with him at Tennessee

Judy Gill Milford

Tech. He is even sending the bus ticket. I can't wait! I think that this is the most exciting thing that has ever happened to me.

* * * *

Homecoming weekend at Tennessee Tech was a disaster! I didn't say fifty words all weekend and I know he didn't have a good time. I talked to him a lot at Junaluska but that was when he was Rose Leigh's friend and I didn't think he would look at me. At homecoming, I was afraid of saying something stupid so I couldn't think of anything—anything at all. Why can't I talk to boys?

* * * *

I have decided to go into elementary education. I never wanted to be a teacher but right now it seems the most logical thing to do. I like English, math, music, art. I don't like any one thing enough to focus on it to the exclusion of everything else. What makes more sense than to get an elementary teaching certificate? That way I can do a lot of different things I enjoy. Besides Mama says that teaching is a good profession for a woman to be in.

* * * *

I have done something really stupid. I bought Pat a Christmas present but I didn't have enough money to

Are You Sure This Is Mine?

buy one for any of the other girls. When I found out Ruth Ann had something for me, I gave her the book of poetry Jimmy Jones gave me last year. She likes poetry so I thought she would like to have one. The bad thing is that I erased my name from the inside and acted like I bought it for her. When she asked me what happened to my book, I told her I took it home. She has pretty clothes and almost everything she wants. I thought she would laugh at me behind my back if I gave her a used book. Now, she is probably laughing because I am so stupid. I think she knows the truth. Why didn't I have the courage to tell her that I was giving her my favorite book?

* * * *

I went out with Robby again this New Year's Eve. We doubled with Jim and Gail just like last year. The other time I went with him I thought that I only wanted him for a friend. For some reason it is different this time. I feel comfortable with him—like I can be me without worrying about saying the right thing or making him think I'm stupid. And he knows exactly what he is going to do when he gets out of school. He will be a CPA when he passes the exam. I never thought I would fall in love with a Catholic but right now that doesn't worry me. Everything seems exactly right.

* * * *

Judy Gill Milford

"Whither thou goest, I will go; and where thou lodgest, I will lodge. Thy people shall be my people and thy God, my God"—Mama read that verse from the first chapter of the Book of Ruth so many times through the years. Would she still have quoted it to me if she had known where it would lead me? Mama's belief in that verse is making it much easier for me to marry Rob because I know that deep down she understands that I must marry in his church if he cannot marry in mine. I must go to church with him and try to accept as many of his beliefs as I can.

For months we have been watching the papers for news of changes made by the pope. We are still hoping for some revisions within the Catholic church in regard to mixed marriages but so far it looks as if they won't come soon enough for us.

I know that it is hard for Mama and Daddy to accept the fact that we will have to marry in Cairo at St. Patrick's. It really isn't fair. Weddings are always at the bride's church and I know God would consider us just as married at Wickliffe Methodist as at St. Patrick's. It is our intention and what is inside us that counts.

* * * *

I bought a paperback book at the Lambuth library book sale tonight called *Understanding the Catholic Faith* by Rev. John O'Brien. I thought that it would help me to understand Rob's faith but parts of it make me mad. The worst part is at the very begin-

Are You Sure This Is Mine?

ning. He speaks of the Catholic church being the "one true church." I was taught that all Christians belong to the same church—the body of believers in Christ. We even say that in the Apostles' Creed every Sunday. "I believe in the Holy Catholic Church" meaning the universal church. Rev. O'Brien says that a Catholic sins against his faith by taking part in non-Catholic worship. I don't see how that could be a sin. There are things a lot worse than participating in another Christian service that a person could worry about.

* * * *

Spring is bursting forth everywhere. Trees are greening, flowers are blooming and I am in love. This morning on the way to class even birds called our names. "Judy and Rob, Judy and Rob," I heard them chirp. The whole world is beautiful and new.

* * * *

Mama and Daddy like Rob a lot and I think they know that he is the only one I have ever really loved, but it is still hard for them knowing that I must sign a paper promising to raise our children Catholic. I think it is the idea of my not having a choice that bothers them more than anything. It bothers me a little, but then I look at Rob and think, "This is the man I love—the one I have chosen to spend the rest of my life with." Admiring and respecting him as I do, can

Judy Gill Milford

our children possibly be cheated by being raised in the same faith that he has? I don't know why I am even worrying about this. I have always wanted children so much that I probably won't be able to have any at all.

* * * *

Rob's aunt Bee fixed dinner for us tonight at her place. She and Fonnie don't have any children so Rob is like her own son. She and Fonnie rent an apartment in an old house and have lots of interesting old things. She is cute and tells the funniest stories. We had a real nice time. I think she is as excited about the wedding as I am.

* * * *

Rob and I went to St. Patrick's tonight with Martha Wilson so that she could see the organ she will be playing for our wedding. Her son, Brett, came along with her and looked around while she was playing. He is close to Chip's age, six or seven. He was curious about everything. As we were leaving he said, "You know, I think I could really like this church if I just knew some of its secrets." I guess I feel a little like Brett. There are still so many "secrets" about the Catholic church that I do not know.

* * * *

Are You Sure This Is Mine?

I can't believe that we got married before Jim and Gail. They have been going together so long. The wedding was almost everything I could have dreamed of. I wish the priest looked a little more like he was saying something meaningful. He said the most important words of my life like they were boring to him. This is the happiest I have ever been in my life. So far we like living in Memphis, but it is a lot different from Wickliffe.

* * * *

I got a phone call from Memphis City Schools. I have a job! I will go to Memphis State for a three week crash course in Special Education. I have to choose between a class of Trainable Mentally Retarded children across town and a class of Educable Mentally Retarded at Florida Street School. Florida Street is so close to our apartment that Rob can drop me by the school on his way to work.

* * * *

As part of this three-week training session I am observing Special Ed classes all over the city. I am learning to go everywhere on the city bus system. This small town girl is learning her way around in the big city.

* * * *

Judy Gill Milford

I have my class now. Florida Street is a pretty big school, about 1500 students for grades 1-6. There are no white kids at all. Out of forty-five teachers only two are white besides myself, and I don't have anything in common with them. I have ten students, ten and eleven years old. They don't have any regular text books and they are at different levels, so I spend hours every night writing lesson plans while Rob studies for the CPA exam.

* * * *

I started out all wrong. I thought that if I walked into a classroom, loved the kids and really wanted to help them everything would be all right. I have never had to discipline before. When I tell them to be seated or to be quiet, no one listens. They call each other names and today one of the boys wrote bad words on the window. I didn't know what to do. I don't know if those words are acceptable here or not. Maybe the rules here are different.

* * * *

I don't know what I would do without Mrs. Dortch and Willie B., the two other special ed. teachers. They are such a big help to me, and so patient with me. I'm sure they wish they had gotten an experienced teacher instead of me. Willie even had Marvin transferred to her class because he was one of my biggest problems.

Are You Sure This Is Mine?

Willie and Mrs. Dortch make teaching look so easy. In my class everything goes wrong.

* * * *

My class is out of control. They call each other "nigger" and "mashed potato head" (whatever that means) and talk about each other's mother, family and whole generation. Nothing I do calms them down. A lot of the teachers have paddles. The kids respect that; they expect it, but I don't think I could spank a child. It doesn't seem to be the right answer.

* * * *

We have one black man who teaches here. Some of the students slashed his tires. That surprises me. I thought he would be their favorite. Willie and Mrs. Dortch said that so many of the children do not have father figures in their homes that they do not know how to relate to a man. I guess that makes sense but I would never have thought of it.

* * * *

Rob and I have decided to try to have a baby. I think he was hoping for us to get a little more money before I stopped working but he is about to get drafted. Neither of us wants him to go to Vietnam. I couldn't be happier about our decision. For as long

Judy Gill Milford

as I can remember one of the things I have wanted most in life is to have babies. I have always known that probably I would not be able to because I wanted it so badly. You just don't get things you want most, do you?

* * * *

I have a student named Richard in my EMRII class. His last name is Ivory but his skin in more like ebony —dark, smooth and shiny. He is small and wiry with large well-formed lips and slanting black eyes that seem to dart. He is always hungry, eager to get an apple core or leftover sucker from the trash can when my back is turned. My own hunger leaves me when I sit next to him at lunch in the cafeteria. The fat-back sandwiches that he brings in his lunch don't look very appetizing.

* * * *

Rob gave me the most beautiful pair of red leather shoes for Christmas. Until now all I could ever afford was a pair of basic black for winter and a pair of white or bone for spring and summer. Every day that I wear my new shoes, I set them carefully under my desk and switch to loafers for comfort when my feet start to hurt.

Today, Richard got behind my desk and slipped his dirt-encrusted feet into my shoes. The other children

Are You Sure This Is Mine?

laughed and made fun as he tried to walk around. I don't know if my shoes will ever be the same.

* * * *

I've never been a quitter so I will hold on until the end of the year, but sometimes I wonder how I will make it. I found a sentence in a book that has become my motto for now, "When you come to the end of your rope, tie a knot and hold on." I have done such a terrible job as teacher of this class. I am a failure at twenty-two. I wonder what can come next when I did such a poor job so soon? Without Rob's support I really couldn't make it.

Judy Gill Milford

II

. . . so that by his death he could take away all the power of the devil, who had power over death, and set free all those who had been held in slavery all their lives by the fear of death. (Hebrews 2:16)

FOR the first time today I held our child, the first miracle created through our love. I can't believe that anyone has felt like this before. At the same time, I know that every mother must. I feel like love was born the instant that I looked at these perfect little toes and fingernails. With her lying on my stomach alive and soft, it's hard to believe that she could have come from me, grown in me all those months. I knew before her birth that she was loved but this is different, so different than I thought it would be. In spite of the emptiness, the flatness of my stomach, I am full to overflowing—almost as if the space once occupied by her inside of me now holds a special love containing pride, hope, dreams, contentment. Could God have felt such love when he first looked

Are You Sure This Is Mine?

on his creation? Having a baby really makes you act like a fool—like you are unique and everything is starting with you.

* * * *

Beth is a thumbsucker. The first time she put her thumb in her mouth she looked so cute that Rob and I sat there smiling. A lady stopped me in the store today and said, "I bet she's a good baby. Thumbsuckers are always good babies. . . ." She is right. I guess it's because they always have something with them to make them happy.

* * * *

Well, we really have a surprise. I was always so afraid that I couldn't have babies and here we are having another one. The thing that bothers me about being pregnant again is that I don't want people to say, "Oh, what did you expect, she married a Catholic." Being a Catholic has nothing to do with this baby we are having.

* * * *

The closer it gets to time for the baby, the more I wonder how we can be fair. We enjoy Beth so much and are having such fun watching her learn. Every

Judy Gill Milford

day is interesting. How can we possibly love this new baby as much as we do her? I'm scared, but no one knows.

* * * *

I hope we have a boy this time. I know the mother doesn't determine the sex of the child but it took my mom so long to have a boy I cannot imagine myself with one.

* * * *

It's a boy! It really is. We are naming him Christopher. I have always loved that name just like I loved "Beth" from the time I saw *Little Women* when I was in third grade. They brought him in just now and laid him in my arms. I look him over and feel his warmth, rub his skinny little leg. How could I have ever doubted?

Chris, second child, you are special. Lying here asleep in reddish face and wrinkled skin you have given me something no other could. You have taught me an exciting mystery in these first moments I have held you, and I love you so!

* * * *

This morning I gave blood at the hospital in Paducah for Grandma Hollenback. She has cancer of the

Are You Sure This Is Mine?

liver. The doctor said there is nothing to be done. He is not even going to operate. Her skin is yellow. She doesn't know what's wrong and they've decided not to tell her. I guess they think it will be easier for her but if I thought there was something wrong with me and no one talked about it, I would want to scream.

* * * *

We are going to the Smokies for a few days of vacation. Beth and Chris are too small for us to take a long trip. We wouldn't go far with Grandma Hollenback so sick anyway. I keep thinking this may be the last trip I get to take with my family. I may never live to see them grow up. I found a lump in my left breast the other day. No one would guess that I am terrified. I smile and talk to Rob and play with the children like nothing is wrong. When no one is around, I look in the mirror and see *death* glaring back at me.

* * * *

I made a doctor's appointment as soon as we got back from the Smokies. By the time I got to the doctor, the lump was gone. I feel silly now, but I was so scared. I don't want anyone else to raise our children. No one could tell them what I want them to know, or love them the way I do.

* * * *

Judy Gill Milford

I am having second thoughts about this thumb-sucking business. To some people it means we are not good parents. They think Beth would not have to resort to her thumb if all her needs were being met.

* * * *

Grandma Hollenback had a peaceful death, I think. She didn't have to suffer a lot of pain like some people with cancer do. I wonder if she knew close to the end that we were all tiptoeing around the truth. At the funeral, Grandpa, who never gave her any joy in life, now wears a grieving face for all the little old ladies who lay their sympathies at his feet like baskets of fresh cut flowers. He scoops them up and wears them proudly, nodding solemnly as supporters remark on his many years of wedded "bliss."

* * * *

With my own children I am learning what I didn't know before. If I put Beth to bed, I cannot change my mind and let her up in a few minutes. If I do that she will soon learn that she can pressure me into change on any issue. Be gentle, but firm. She has to know from the beginning that I mean what I say.

* * * *

Are You Sure This Is Mine?

It is funny to wake up one day and realize that you aren't going to shake the world with your achievements. The songs, the poems, the oil paintings, where are they? It's later than you think. Mediocrity is stifling. Fight back. It is not too late, is it? Sure you love your husband and children, but love is not a limitation. It is an expanse. Who says you are confined to mopping floors and ironing baby clothes? Organization, motivation, determination—where are they? Don't give up yet. You have wasted a lot of time but if you are lucky, you have a lot left. You won't know until you try. Don't be so conservative. Venture out.

* * * *

O.K. so you had a bad morning. Straighten up and stop feeling sorry for yourself. What would you do if you really had problems? Know when you are well off. Look around you and give thanks. You know you aren't as independent as you think.

* * * *

Live every moment and give thanks. Are children the only ones who know God? Why do we as adults become so independent and all-knowing until there is a crisis?

* * * *

Judy Gill Milford

People are created equal but they are not born that way. As much as we would like to think otherwise, people are not born to equal opportunities.

* * * *

Another thing about Beth's thumb is her teeth. Will it damage her teeth? I once knew a girl who sucked her thumb until she was twelve and her teeth stuck out. What if Beth never stops? Will she take it to kindergarten, the prom, down the aisle?

* * * *

This morning Rob and I went to church at different times because Beth and Chris were sick. While I was there, the priest passed a petition and told us to sign it. They are sending it to a congressman protesting an abortion issue. I just passed it to the person on my left. There's something about being told to do something that will not allow me to do it. If he had instructed us to read it and follow our consciences or do as Christ would do, it would have been different, but he said, "sign," so I passed. I don't really understand why I am so determined to make my own decisions. I don't like to think of myself as stubborn, but maybe I am.

* * * *

Are You Sure This Is Mine?

I am down to 110 pounds. I love the way I feel with no fat (maybe I should say not much fat). We went home this weekend to visit Mom and Dad and Dorothy and John. At church in Wickliffe several people asked me if I am sick. They are not used to seeing me this way. I don't know why they think I'm sick; it feels great.

* * * *

Rob and I went to the drive-in tonight and saw *Cool Hand Luke*. I had little in common with Paul Newman as Cool-hand Luke throughout most of the film. Mistreated and misunderstood, Luke tried repeatedly to escape from a prison farm or chain gang when he wasn't swallowing dozens of hard-boiled eggs, ogling a voluptuous car-washer, or singing, "I don't care if it rains or freezes, as long as I have my plastic Jesus sitting on the dashboard of my car." Not much for me to identify with there, but toward the end, I was Cool-hand Luke in that empty church calling out, "O.K. God, if you are real, where are you?" Isn't that what I've been saying for years? What I wouldn't give to have God answer me—to show me he is real.

* * * *

Judy Gill Milford

I am consumed by fear—again. How many times in the past three or four years since we have had children have I been convinced that I am dying? Why would anyone with a loving husband, healthy children and a nice home be as miserable as I am? I have everything a person needs to be happy, and I am happy. Yet repeatedly, I try to resign myself to the probability of dying—of not being around to watch my children grow up. In my mind I play, replay the scene—the one where the doctor tells me that it is too late. That I have six months, two months, one month to live. I try to prepare myself, try to imagine exactly how I will feel when he tells me there is no hope.

And then comes the feeling of foolishness and relief when I find there is nothing wrong, at least nothing life-threatening. How many times have I lived this?

* * * *

Rob doesn't know how upset I am. I tell him everything (almost everything), but not this. He would think I am crazy. Anybody would. Maybe I am. A person would have to be crazy to create problems for herself when there are none, wouldn't she?

* * * *

So many times I have said to God, "If you are there, please let me know, show me." It is possible that he

Are You Sure This Is Mine?

is doing just that? This crippling fear of mine shows me that I am not as independent and self-sufficient as I try to be. God is there. I need him and he is reaching out to me.

* * * *

I have been released from the fear that bound me! I turned all my pain over to him and it is no longer mine. A weight has been lifted from me. I have perfect peace for the first time in so long. The inner torment is actually gone. I can actually enjoy life and my wonderful children.

* * * *

Speaking of children, I love them, but let's face it, there are a couple of things that I would change if I could:

1. Milk spills. I would have the children wait until the milk is cleaned up before asking for a new glass. I can handle the spill and the mess, but when they cry for a new glass while I'm still on hands and knees, I almost lose patience.

2. Illness. I'd get them to the bathroom before they throw up. They are good about waking but usually get as far as our bedroom carpet.

Judy Gill Milford

Cleaning carpet on hands and knees at 3:00 A.M. is a real tribute to motherhood.

3. Batteries. The children would always replace those little protective covers that hold batteries in place. It wouldn't be bad if they didn't have battery operated games or toys at all. Those things rarely outlast their first set of batteries.

4. Soggy washcloths. My husband never drops a washcloth in the tub. Why do I let our children get away with it? If they had to gather those things up for the laundry, they would quit, wouldn't they?

Part Two

The Search Continues

III

And for anyone who is in Christ, there is a new creation; the old creation is gone, and now the new one is here. (II Cor. 5:17)

I AM going to talk to Father Atkinson about taking instruction. Since I am going through this renewal period, I want to see if I can accept Catholicism. The children are getting older and it is hard for me to answer their questions knowing that some of my answers may be different from Rob's. Besides, I've been going to the Catholic church with him for almost five years. I don't really feel Methodist anymore. There are some things about the Catholic church that I actually like better.

* * * *

Father Atkinson and I are meeting with one other woman who is interested in becoming Catholic. We are going through the book *Life of Christ* step by step. We have discussions and can ask questions about

Judy Gill Milford

anything we don't understand. I have a lot of questions so I'm glad there aren't many there. I would probably be embarrassed to ask if there were more than three or four.

* * * *

I like the idea of purgatory. It never did seem fair that a person would go to hell if he was good, or if he did not join the right church.

One thing that still bothers me is that the Catholic church says Jesus had no brothers or sisters. Matthew 28:10 refers to brothers when Jesus said, "Do not be afraid; go and tell my brothers that they must leave for Galilee; they will see me there." And Mark 3:32-34: "A crowd was sitting around him at the time the message was passed to him, 'Your mother and brothers and sisters are outside asking for you.' He replied, 'Who are my mother and my brothers?' And looking around at those sitting in a circle about him, he said, 'Here are my mother and my brothers. Anyone who does the will of God, that person is my brother and sister and mother.'" The explanation given by the Catholic church doesn't quite clear up the confusion, but it isn't an issue worth making a big deal about.

Another thing that is different in the Catholic church is communion. In the Methodist church when we took communion, the bread and wine were

Are You Sure This Is Mine?

symbols of the body and blood of Christ. The Catholic church believes that the bread and wine actually become the body and blood of Christ. Father Atkinson helped me to understand. If we truly believe that God is all-powerful, then we have to believe that with him all things are possible. Therefore, to say that he could not change bread and wine is taking away some of his power. Knowing that he can, there is no need to question it.

* * * *

Father Atkinson said that the Catholic church would accept my baptism from when I joined the Methodist church when I was seven. It is valid because I remember making the choice. It would bother me if he told me my other baptism was no good.

* * * *

Ever since Chris was born we have considered our family complete but now that I am joining the Catholic church, and everything else is right with our lives, it seems natural for us to have another baby. Beth really wants a little sister but I told her we won't know until it gets here.

* * * *

Judy Gill Milford

Beth is disappointed that there is no sister but she and Chris are fascinated with Robby. At 6 lb. 14 oz. he is our smallest baby.

* * * *

We are moving to Paducah so that Rob can go into partnership in a small CPA firm there. We will have more time since it will take him five minutes to get to work instead of the forty-five that it takes here. This is something he has wanted to do for some time.

* * * *

In the church bulletin this morning I read about a need for foster parents for very young babies. I would like to do that but since we are moving to Paducah soon there is no need to check into it. When I mentioned it to Rob, he was not in favor of it anyway. He thinks I would get too attached to the babies. He may be right but they would surely benefit from the love I could give them. We have so much, we need to share with someone.

* * * *

J.J., our cock-o-poo, has breast cancer and has had surgery. She will have follow-up treatments. I have to

Are You Sure This Is Mine?

take her to the vet every day for a week or two. The big C haunts me every place I turn.

* * * *

The Catholic church here in Paducah is different than it was in Memphis. Here the church is more like the Catholic church was years ago. I thought it was supposed to be the same all over, but I guess that is impossible. I wonder if I would have been ready to join the church if I had gone through instruction here.

* * * *

Beth and Chris are going to the public school. I really felt that it was important for them to go to school with all children so that they wouldn't think that Catholicism was all that there is. I want them to respect the religious beliefs of all people, but especially of their grandparents and other relatives on my side of the family. I get the feeling that some of our Catholic friends think we are terrible for not sending them to Catholic school. I've heard a lot of quarreling and complaints coming from the Catholic school parents so I'm not sure whether the environment is any more Christian than the public school in some respects.

* * * *

Judy Gill Milford

In the church bulletin this morning are ink cartoon-type drawings depicting different methods of abortion. Beth, Chris and Robby saw them as we were riding home from church and began to ask questions. I wish they would use another method for teaching anti-abortion. Why emphasize the negative with children of this age? They have no understanding of why a knife would be cutting a baby into fifteen or twenty pieces. Isn't it better to encourage reverence for life? to teach that life is beautiful and each person loved?

* * * *

Aunt Bee is giving us some of her favorite books for Beth, Chris and Robby. Three of them are by Gene Stratton-Porter. I intended not to read them. They are so old (printed early 1900s) that I didn't think they could have anything to say to me. What a loss I would have had, if I had not. They are uplifting stories. In fact, I enjoyed them so much I have read all that the library had. I even read *The Song of the Cardinal*, a love story of a bird and its mate. In her books I am transported to a land that no longer exists, but one in which I would gladly live. It is refreshing to read a romantic story that leaves everything to the imagination. Gene Stratton-Porter says:

> To my way of thinking and working, the greatest service a piece of fiction can do any reader is to leave him with a higher ideal of life than he had

Are You Sure This Is Mine?

> when he began. If in one small degree it shows him where he can be a gentler, saner, cleaner, kindlier man, it is a wonder-working book. If it opens his eyes to one beauty in nature he never saw for himself and leads him one step toward God of the Universe, it is a beneficial book, for one step into the miracle of nature leads to that long walk.[1]

I like her wholesome approach.

* * * *

I am going to a new non-denominational Bible study. I want to read and learn more about God's word but nothing is offered at St. Thomas More Church. The woman who wrote the series I am attending comes on a little strong in my opinion, but I agree with a lot that she says. We are studying Paul's Letter to the Philippians. I never knew it was so good. In Chapter 1:20-25 Paul says:

> My one hope and trust is that I shall never have to admit defeat, but that now as always I shall have the courage for Christ to be glorified in my body, whether by my life or by my death. Life to me, of course, is Christ, but then again, if living in this body means doing work which is having good results—I do not know what I should choose. I am caught in this dilemma: I want to be gone and be with Christ, which would be very much the bet-

Judy Gill Milford

ter, but for me to stay alive in this body is a more urgent need for your sake.

In chapter 3:10,11, Paul tells us: "All I want is to know Christ and the power of his resurrection and to share his sufferings by reproducing the pattern of his death."

And in Chapter 4, verses 6-7:

Don't worry about anything, but in all your prayers ask God for what you need, always asking him with a thankful heart. And God's peace, which is far beyond human understanding, will keep your hearts and minds safe, in Christ Jesus.

How I envy Paul's love and devotion! I want to love Jesus more than life, but I love life so much that I'm not sure that I could ever reach that degree of devotion.

Another part of Paul's letter that I must remember, 2:6-11, tells us the attitude of Christ. This gives me important guidelines:

He always had the very nature of God,
But he did not think that by force he should try to become equal with God.
Instead, of his own free will he gave it all up,
And took the nature of a servant.
He was born like man, he appeared in human likeness;
He was humble and walked the path of obedience to death—his death on the cross.

Are You Sure This Is Mine?

> For this reason God raised him to the highest place above,
> And gave him the name that is greater than any other name,
> So that all beings in heaven, and on earth, and in the world below
> Will fall on their knees,
> In honor of the name of Jesus,
> And all will openly proclaim that Jesus Christ is the Lord
> to the glory of God the Father.

Is this the same Bible I read when I was a girl—the Bible that didn't make sense, was boring? A mystery is unraveling on these pages and it is exciting to see how everything fits together. Every time I read I see something I never saw before. The New Testament is still a lot more interesting than the Old. With time and study maybe I can understand it all. I think that God gives us wisdom to understand things that were once impossible.

Judy Gill Milford

IV

Whatever you ask for my name I will do, so that the Father may be glorified in the Son. If you ask for anything in my name, I will do it. (John 14:13,14)

We know that by turning everything to their good God co-operates with all those who love him, with all those that he has called according to his purpose. (Romans 8:28)

CHARLIE called this morning from Georgia. Marilyn died. I knew she had cancer and that it was bad, but I just didn't think she would die. I feel like it was my fault. I told her I would pray for her—and I did pray, some. Why didn't I pray more; why didn't I pray unceasingly? Now, she will never see Chuck and Page grow up. And they will never remember the vibrant, healthy, funny young woman I roomed with in college. We are told that God answers prayers, but we are also told that all things happen according to God's purpose. Would, could

Are You Sure This Is Mine?

my prayers have made any difference? Oh God, there are some things that I just don't understand.

* * * *

Pope Paul VI died of a heart attack August 6. Pope John Paul has taken his place.

* * * *

The new pope John Paul has already died after only thirty-four days as pope. I had a good feeling about him as pope. Sometimes, I don't understand God's plan for the world. I guess I expect him to run things the way I would if I were God.

* * * *

A Polish priest has been elected and has taken the name Pope John Paul II. It is very unusual to have a pope who is not Italian, but it may be beneficial to have a pope from a Communist country.

* * * *

One of the books I checked out from the library this week was poetry by Susan Polis Schutz. It is very different from the poetry we studied in school. In fact, it is not like poetry at all. While I was reading I suddenly knew that it would feel very natural for me to

Judy Gill Milford

write the way she does. Ever since high school I have been so conscious of all the rules I learned: never begin sentences with *and* or *but*, rarely begin sentences with *I*, make sure sentences are complete (subject and verb), etc. It was never fun to write, just work. Here is someone writing in a published book just the way she thinks or talks—the way I think. I love the idea. I am writing feelings I have carried for years. I have never felt so free. It will be nice to have the things I am writing. I often think Beth, Chris and Robby don't know the real me—what I believe in, what is important to me. Now, when I am gone, something of me will remain.

* * * *

It was one of those duty masses—one from which you expect nothing. We were visiting Jim and Gail for the weekend and attending church in their parish —in a hurry for church to be over so that we could get on with our visit. I managed to get through the homily without paying much attention but a song drew me in. It's hard to believe that sometimes we receive a blessing from a simple song. "Jesus, my Lord, my God, my all! How can I love thee as I ought?" I couldn't even tell who wrote it but from the first line I knew that it could have been me. The words were the verbalization of a plea from my inner being. "Oh, make us love thee more and more." Isn't

Are You Sure This Is Mine?

that the plea that I have been living and continue to live? Someone else must have experienced this very feeling before me to have written those words. Knowing that does not solve my problem, my feeling of inadequacy, but sometimes it does help to know that we are not the only one.

* * * *

King-Size Bed

After twelve years of marriage
in a double bed,
we bought a king
so large and firm.
We stretched and lounged—
hardly ever touched.
What luxury
night after night
tossing and turning
with plenty of room.
One night our youngest child crawled in
awakened by the cold
and we were not crowded—
that was nice.
But then we went out of town,
visited friends
and slept in a double again.
That night I realized

Judy Gill Milford

the comforting weight of his leg
   slung over mine,
the peaceful warmth and smell
   of his closeness,
the reassurance of his rhythmic
   breathing by my side,
and the ease with which
   two people drift apart.

* * * *

Last week on a hike, Chris, Robby, Beth and I found something on an old piece of wood that looked like a dried up snail without its shell. We put it in a baby food jar, brought it home and set it on the shelf. We had forgotten about it until this morning when we found that a beautiful, perfectly formed spicebush swallowtail butterfly had emerged. Struggling to be free in the small jar, its wings were melting into the condensation on the glass. It was damaged beyond chance for survival. Aren't many people born very much like that butterfly, trapped beyond any chance to break out?

* * * *

My entire purpose in being is to help other people. When the time comes, those people will benefit more

Are You Sure This Is Mine?

from my death than from my life. I will no doubt be transferred.

* * * *

Sometimes I snap at him,
This ten-year-old,
This middle child of ours.
Why does he infuriate me so,
This blue-eyed sprinkle of freckles
With turned-up pixie smile?
I build a wall —
Not vast completely shutting
Out love, but a small one
That partly shields my face.
He must not see how totally
I stand in awe of him
For if he did, I would be
More vulnerable.
He is stubborn, sure, a mystery.
I want much for him.
How far should I go?
If he were clay
I would want to preserve
His natural beauty
Yet enhance it,
Lend the knowledge of my experiences,
But not press too hard

Judy Gill Milford

Lest I make a dent or cause a crack
That would affect a total change.
A little gentle molding —
Is all he needs.

* * * *

Bub was always one of my favorite uncles. He let me feed chickens and introduced me to his friend, a toad that lived beneath his front door step. We shared the friendship of that toad for years. Once he let me see his room, a mysterious attic space sparcely furnished with bed and books that smelled of unfinished wood and tobacco—intriguing to a four-year-old.

I saw Bub Saturday night all dressed up in suit and tie, but I remember him most often in overalls—filling his pipe from a can of Prince Albert (or was it Sir Walter Raleigh) with his blue eyes blinking from behind those wire frames he wore when I was young. He never married—lived alone for years. I'd pass his house and think, "I'd like to stop." But usually I'm in a hurry so I would drive on by. When I saw him I always said, "Please come by to see us, we'd love to have you."

He died Tuesday—all alone, the way he lived. I wish that just once I had said, "Please come Sunday at 2:00."

* * * *

Are You Sure This Is Mine?

Why do we wait until a person is dead to realize what we can do for them? We always think we have plenty of time left for that sort of thing.

* * * *

At Bub's funeral I watched a relative who wouldn't talk to Bub while he was alive. With crumpled face the mourner stood over the casket and wept. Watching his display of grief I wondered if he was sorry for his treatment of Bub during his lifetime or if the man was merely weeping because Bub's death reminded him of his own mortality.

* * * *

It feels good to be writing. But in a way it scares me. It is like opening the gates of a dam when I don't know if the source is a river or a lake. After one big flood of thought will I be dry? or will I, continuing to feed from tributaries, maintain a steady flowing stream, sometimes full to overflowing, sometimes low, always running on?

* * * *

I'm thirty-five today. I feel younger now than I did when I was seventeen. I ride my bike and run and laugh with only a few things to give me away. The wrinkles at the sides of my eyes, the cracking in my

Judy Gill Milford

knees as I go down stairs—they mean nothing, for my heart is young. It is amazing how the love and trust of a kind and gentle man can let years glide so lightly by. Because of him, I grow, I leap, I fly. He doesn't tie me down—just holds me gently, tenderly in his care.

* * * *

Dorothy is not well. I wish that there were some way to help, but feel totally helpless. I wish she would talk to me. She always says only what she thinks I want to hear. Never admits to being sad, tired or depressed. She smiles, tells me she's fine and compliments me. How can I tell her that someday she can walk in and say, "The kids are too loud" or "Sometimes you make me so mad." Oh, I don't mean that I want her to be rude or uncaring, or that I'm not glad that she cares enough to try. But I don't expect perfection. She can let me glimpse—just glimpse inside, and I'll still love her.

* * * *

Oh, God, I don't understand mental illness. When a person is having emotional problems, it seems that with faith and a willingness to turn the problems over to you, healing would take place. When that doesn't happen, it is hard to understand why. We don't always get physical healing when we ask

Are You Sure This Is Mine?

either, so I guess there are some things we have to accept without understanding.

* * * *

    I love the freshness of early mornings
       cool and crisp as just-picked apples
       caught before they fall from the tree.
    I love the feel of dew-dampened grass
       caressing feet while toes in turn
       explore each moisture-laden
       blade of green.
    I love the sound of birds' first songs
       with their twittering, chirping flight
       betraying their eagerness to get in that
       first hymn of praise for a new day.
    I love the washed-clean smell of early morning
       when all things seem much purer, newer,
       fresher than the night before.
    Overnight, in the quiet of the shadows
    Hope was born.

* * * *

To exchange unkind words with another mother over something as silly as Boy Scout Expo tickets sounds absurd. How did it happen?

    Her words have sharp edges,
    stabbing, stinging, scratching

Judy Gill Milford

I draw back
then venture out again
recoil with discomfort
flinch with pain
Conversation ended
I nurse my wounds
They fester
as I analyze my injuries
These weapons — harmless weapons
what pain they inflict
Will the wounds heal like some
leaving not a trace?
or will the scars like others
be always too painful
to touch?

* * * *

I cannot pass a gravel driveway or a section of gravel road without sitting down to look through the rocks. Usually I go home with a pocketfull. Every rock is special to me. I save some for color, texture, shape or fossil. Some, like geodes, have hidden beauty. People are a lot like rocks. I hardly ever see one that doesn't offer a treasure.

* * * *

I am thankful that Rob still loves me after all these years. Sometimes, I wonder if he always will. How

Are You Sure This Is Mine?

could he love me with all my faults until the end of time? Will he wake up some morning and see all my imperfections before him blocking all he loved before from sight? As he grows older, will his patience wear thin? Will he require that everything be finished off in neat little packages leaving no room for me?

Here I am—mastermind of disorganization, inventor of unfinished projects. He sees me go from room to room never quite finishing what I start, and yet he loves me still.

* * * *

Beth and Chris have a supplementary reading list for a special class. In reading some of their books so that we could talk about them, I have discovered C. S. Lewis and Madeleine L'Engle. Lewis wrote several adult books in addition to *Chronicles of Narnia*. All of the ones that I have read from the library are good. I read the rest of L'Engle's, too. Once I met her characters, I had to keep going back to visit until I knew them all.

* * * *

Why are some Christians close-minded in their judgment of other persons? Don't they know that God works with each of us in his own time? We are none of us in exactly the same place, so we should

Judy Gill Milford

not impose our limitations on another. Why do we expect perfection in others that is absent in ourselves?

* * * *

I wonder if Joyce Kilmer was happy with what he had to say about trees. Although his famous poem is not considered great, it has given a lot of tree-loving, non-poetic people something to say—something to turn to when praising trees. If I had written "Trees," I would believe that I had not and could never say enough. Until there is a way to paint the smell, the sound, the feel of a tree as well as the look with words, all descriptions are inadequate. The joy I feel when I experience a tree is like a bud bursting into blossom. I smell the seasons of the trees and feel the variations of their trunks and know that there are no paints or words to capture the exhilaration.

* * * *

I check out books from the library and take page after page of notes—things I must remember. Most of my notes come from Thomas Merton and St. Augustine, some from C. S. Lewis. I need to own the books so that I can mark the good parts. There are too many passages to write down everything I want to find again.

* * * *

Are You Sure This Is Mine?

I've always wondered what it would be like to serve on a jury. Why did I have to be called right here in the middle of summer when there is so much to do and the children are out of school?

> I was called for jury duty in July
> my favorite outdoor swim and tennis month.
> One civil case involved some nieces and
>   nephews
> who wanted their aunt Martha
> declared incompetent
> to handle her own money.
> Said they had gone to her house
> numerous times when it was terribly untidy.
> She answered the door in her bare feet,
> ate tuna sandwiches for breakfast,
> and sometimes,
> she wasn't even sure what day it was.
> Her family doctor even took the stand
> to say she sometimes acted strange.
> I'm glad that those nieces and nephews
> have no claim on me.

* * * *

I have trouble throwing things away. If I have a long white skirt with giant strawberries on it, I'd better keep it and know exactly where it is in case I need it for the school play in 1998. It's as if a giant hand will point a finger at me from the clouds on that day

Judy Gill Milford

and say judgmentally—"You had one of those, I know you did and you didn't take care of it."

* * * *

I have found another good book at the library, *Christ in Eclipse*. I will have to study it to absorb everything it has to offer. The author tells us that "Christ himself is a revered presence in a depth of the mind that one seldom visits. We might be living in his service, yet not know him any better than we knew him as children. He is not absent, but surely in eclipse."[1] That is a good way to describe the way I feel about my relationship with Christ—in eclipse.

* * * *

Are You Sure This Is Mine?

V

I have been crucified with Christ, and I live now not with my own life but with the life of Christ who lives in me. (Galatians 2:20)

ALL THE time I have been trying to know Christ, looking for him and there he was dwelling within me the whole time. Any strength I have is not my own. It comes from him in me.

* * * *

Tonight, we had some friends over. While we were sitting around talking about religion, Mike remarked that he had never questioned the existence of God. I didn't want to hear that. I thought that the periods of questioning and doubting that I experienced were a normal part of growing up. I envy the security of his position—that of not having doubted. I am much like Thomas. I want to see his hands, put my fingers to his side. I admit that I have learned a lot by question-

Judy Gill Milford

ing, but it seems much easier Mike's way. How blest I would be to believe without seeing.

* * * *

Mom and I went to lunch today for her birthday. The birthday lunches are a nice thing about living closer to our parents. Mom likes to go out to eat and Daddy doesn't. I like being able to have these special lunches with her. Anyway, this morning I went to Kroger to cash a check for our lunch and later discovered I was ten dollars short. I checked with Kroger in case they were over in their cash drawer. I retraced my steps and went through my purse and car two or three times. Nothing. I can't stand doing something like that—losing money. Finally, I realized that all I could do is hope that someone found it that really needed it. Wouldn't it be neat if somebody short on cash came out of Kroger and found my money in the parking lot?

* * * *

Dorothy is in the hospital. Because she had chest pains, they thought at first she was having a heart attack. They have diagnosed pancreatitis. She cannot talk and is in a lot of pain. They have moved her from cardiac to intensive care. Our lives are centered around her, the hospital and visiting hours. We alter-

Are You Sure This Is Mine?

nate between preparing to grieve and preparing to hope that we will not have to.

* * * *

Now, we are part of a new family—the Intensive Care support team. Relatives of other patients gather with us in the waiting room to watch, wait and silently pray. We are bonded together in a special way by this common experience—we are equalized by the illness and probable deaths of our loved ones. I know that God is tending to all of us through this. I can feel a strength and a peace beyond what I normally have.

* * * *

I wish we could communicate with her. She is too sick to write and because of the respirator is unable to speak. I try to talk to her of things but what would I want to say if I were her? It is impossible to know. Prayer is sustaining all of us.

* * * *

Aunt Bee has unintentionally given us a moment of laughter in the midst of all this. She almost caught my kitchen on fire while some of us were at the hospital. She then told the children not to tell John (her brother) because he would think she was not

Judy Gill Milford

helping and send her home to Cairo. I don't know how anyone could have missed the smell of burnt Tupperware when we came in the front door.

* * * *

Dorothy has been in ICU for days now. Our house is full of relatives so Rob and I are sleeping on the den floor. Lying there in the dark talking about his mother's impending death, I learned something incredibly important and having learned, I feel foolish, but wiser. Rob confided to me that he thought of his mother as a saint because of the emotional problems she has had in the past and the suffering she has been through. I was stunned and ashamed to realize that what I viewed as weakness, he saw as strength. It certainly taught me a lesson about the way we view others to realize that while I was thinking how glad he must be that he married someone strong who could handle things, he was busy giving his mother the credit she deserves.

* * * *

We have received a great blessing from God. The doctors told us that because there is no hope, we would have to decide whether to continue with the respirator. Her death came before a decision. I am so thankful. It was not our decision to make and not one I would want to live with. If she could not recover

Are You Sure This Is Mine?

and be a whole person, I think she would have wanted this.

* * * *

Part of me is content with this—the small talk and conversation of the life I lead, happy to be accepted by my friends, willing to drift along. Another part of me wants to stand up and shout, "I'm not bridge, needlepoint, garden clubs and 14K gold chains. I'm Chopin, oak trees, autumn leaves and bare feet." Most of all I'm haunted by the aging face of every child who deserves the chance to be young—and is not getting it.

* * * *

Some problems, I think, are allowed by God to keep me close to him or to get me back on track if I wander. II Corinthians 12:7-10 tells us ". . . I was given a thorn in the flesh, an angel of Satan to beat me and stop me from getting too proud! About this thing, I have pleaded with the Lord three times for it to leave me, but he has said, 'My grace is enough for you, my power is at its best in weakness.'"

When I discovered this lump, I had trouble understanding why it interfered with my peace. Wasn't this the same old problem (fear of death) that I conquered before? Why was I not handling it with more dignity, more faith? Why this fear gnawing in the pit

Judy Gill Milford

of my stomach that I could not control? Yesterday, in the shower, I prayed. If this is from Satan to sidetrack me, I reject it. I will not accept it—it does not exist. If it is from God for a good purpose, I have nothing to worry about. He will give me strength to deal with whatever comes my way. I have regained my peace. Thanks to God.

* * * *

A February snow has dusted the ground. Passing a neighbor's yard today I noticed a blackjack oak with leaves hanging stubbornly to the bough like old men long past caring. Shriveled and dry with age they hang forgotten with presence barely acknowledged, beauty rarely recalled. I wonder why they stay so long.

* * * *

My time is running out. It has been since my birth, but sometimes I wonder if I could have, should have been two separate persons. There is the total woman, total wife-mother, loving my children and my man, cooking for them, caring for their needs—contented.

Then there is the other me—the one with need to be alone to read, write and meditate. To waste an hour looking at a textured twig or leaf. The balance that I

Are You Sure This Is Mine?

keep presents a panic—a sense of urgency. Will there be time to do it all—to live both?

* * * *

It is difficult to tell the difference between problems the Lord sends to strengthen me, and the things the devil does to tempt me. Does the outcome show the difference? If I succumb, was it temptation and if not, a strengthening device? Actually, God does not send any of these hardships—he merely allows them.

* * * *

The first cool breeze is blowing now across September. Most trees stand proudly green and full of life. I don't understand why some leaves hurl themselves like wreckless young skydivers to the ground. I am angered by their irreverent eagerness to leave the tree.

* * * *

We got a call from John. Bee died suddenly this morning while Fonnie was in the shower. We had no warning at all. I think she would have preferred this passing to a long illness.

* * * *

Judy Gill Milford

At the funeral the minister read II Corinthians 5:1-3, "For we know that when the tent that we live in on earth is folded up, there is a house built by God for us, an everlasting home not made by human hands, in the heavens. In this present state, it is true, we groan as we wait with longing to put on our heavenly home over the other."

I think Bee would have been pleased.

* * * *

Did I really run that stop sign, the one I stop at four or five times every day? The policeman said I did—said it was a rolling stop and that wasn't good enough. I don't know. I played it and replayed it in my mind. It was a stop to me. Maybe it was a good thing it happened though. That ticket may have saved my life—or someone else's. If I was getting careless about my driving, the ticket was just the thing to make me alert again. The siren, the policeman in my rearview mirror, realizing he wanted *me* to pull over, and the embarrassment of knowing that all passersby were curious to know what I had done. Yes, I will pay the fine and wonder if God sends us these warnings now and then—if we pay attention.

I am having difficulty with this Bible study course on John. The author of the course said she intends to lead us to the truth only, not tell us what to believe; but in this course without realizing it, she is telling

Are You Sure This Is Mine?

us. It is confusing for me because on this one point her teaching goes against what I have always believed. It will take study and prayer to work this one out.

* * * *

Judy Gill Milford

VI

The spirit is willing, but the flesh is weak. Again, a second time he went away and prayed; "My Father," he said, "if this cup cannot pass by without my drinking it, your will be done!" (Matthew 26: 41,42)

AFTER ten years there is life growing inside of me—again. I never thought that there would be another baby. I thought that part of my life was over. I worry that something will be wrong with this one. Maybe this is what God had in mind for me when he called me back to him. Maybe he knew that it would take strength that only he could give to deal with a handicapped child. We have decided against amniocentesis. God wants us to have this baby regardless. And the amnio itself presents a risk, too. A lot of things could be wrong that wouldn't even show on the test. What a feeling, carrying this mystery inside with no clue to its well-being.

* * * *

Are You Sure This Is Mine?

We told Beth, Chris and Robby about the baby. They were surprised, but I think excited, too. Of course, Beth wants a sister. She says two brothers are more than enough.

* * * *

I am surprised at the difference in this pregnancy. Having a baby at thirty-eight is not as easy as at twenty-eight. I thought I would feel the same. I'm in pretty good shape, aren't I?

* * * *

Yesterday, Chris, Robby and some of the other neighborhood boys were going to camp out in our side yard. They had tents up and everything was ready. While some of the boys were waiting for Khoury League baseball to be over, Jay was hit by a car. He was injured so badly there was no chance for survival. The boys are stunned. So is everyone else in the neighborhood. We all knew that Audubon and Sunset was a dangerous intersection. It is impossible to see cars coming over that little hill. We are petitioning for a stop sign. Why did a little boy have to die to get it?

* * * *

Every time we can't find Chris or one of the other boys in the neighborhood, we know now that they

Judy Gill Milford

are talking to Jay's mom. She has been so courageous, encouraging the boys to keep coming to her house since he died. It would be easy for them to cut themselves off from her for fear of saying the wrong thing. I don't think I could do as well as she has.

* * * *

Well, we have another boy. I am not surprised. I could not imagine a little girl in the house. Maybe it has been too long. He is a perfect, beautiful baby (although the children say he looks like E.T.). Everything seems to be all right with him. For the entire pregnancy, I was sure that something was very wrong. Now, I look into those penetrating eyes like pools of darkest ink and realize the miracle again. He acts as if he was born starving. The first time they brought him to nurse, he clamped on tight with no coaxing and wouldn't turn loose until I pried him off.

* * * *

I keep thinking about Jay's mom, and I don't want to. Here I am overjoyed at the birth of a third healthy son and her only son has just been killed. How can I even face her? Surely, she must see the injustice of it and be angry at me—at someone. I know that I would be.

* * * *

Are You Sure This Is Mine?

She brought a gift for Will and seemed happy for us. I almost feel guilty. Wouldn't she just want to scream into the silence of her lonely house?

* * * *

For the first time I have someone coming once a week to help clean. Rob suggested it when he was in the hospital for gall bladder surgery. I never thought I would have someone clean for me, but it is a great feeling having the entire house clean at once. I was never able to do everything in one day.

* * * *

Dorothy H. is cleaning for me. She does a good job and I like her a lot, but maybe I wasn't cut out to have a cleaning lady. I feel guilty—guilty that I have nice things that she cannot afford, guilty that I did not have the house cleaner before she came to clean it, guilty if I ask her to do something she doesn't ordinarily do. I spend half my time apologizing.

* * * *

A friend and I had a discussion about priests marrying. At first my sympathies were with married priests, but many Catholics are very much against it. I was forced to examine the other side of the issue. Although it is very romantic to think of a priest find-

Judy Gill Milford

ing love and marrying, breaking a promise with the church would be equivalent to me breaking my marriage vows and seeking a new partner, or worse, because I found a new partner that I desired. I think there is a good chance that priests will eventually be allowed to marry. According to scripture it would be acceptable. I Corinthians 7:25-28: "About remaining celibate, I have no directions from the Lord but give my own opinion as one who, by the Lord's mercy, has stayed faithful. . . . If you are tied to a wife do not look for freedom; if you are free of a wife, then do not look for one. But if you marry, it is no sin, and it is not a sin for a young girl to get married," and verse 33 tells us, "An unmarried man can devote himself to the Lord's affairs, all he need worry about is pleasing the Lord; but a married man has to bother about the world's affairs and devote himself to pleasing his wife: he is torn two ways."

* * * *

To my family, Thanksgiving, '82

Thanksgiving '82 approaches and I feel sad. I don't know why. I have so much to give thanks for. Maybe that is why. Joyful sadness. Past Thanksgivings come to mind. Remember '66, our first Thanksgiving as R. and J. Milford? We baked a chicken for the two of us. It looked so funny sitting there in place of the traditional turkey. The next year we stayed in Memphis sharing with friends, afraid to travel so close to the

Are You Sure This Is Mine?

expected arrival of our firstborn. She was late, we could have traveled with ease.

I remember the year I was barely pregnant with Robby. I had a virus and was so afraid that somehow he could be harmed because of it. We were blessed again.

Year after year we had trouble remembering whether it was the year to have noon Thanksgiving at Milfords and evening at Gills or the other way around.

Then came the year we hardly had Thanksgiving at all. Dorothy was in ICU not expected to live. Beth, Chris, Robby and I went to Grandma and Grandpa Gill's to pretend normal Thanksgiving. I think Rob, John and Bee had country ham here. Even that year there was a lot to give thanks for. I was especially thankful for our move to Paducah. We were able to spend a lot of special time at the hospital with Dorothy because we lived so close.

Then the next year—Thanksgiving without Dorothy or Bee. We shared it at Grandma and Grandpa Gill's. I was thankful that John could be a part of sharing there.

1982. We certainly have a lot to be thankful for this year. Beth is such a pretty young woman. So eager to drive, to be grown. I am so proud of her. She is neat, organized, disciplined, self-confident. I see so many good qualities in her that I didn't have myself when I was her age.

Chris has grown this year. All of a sudden I am the

Judy Gill Milford

short mother of an almost grown son. He, too, makes me proud. His friendly face is a joy to see. He is responsible and orderly with his lessons (with only an occasional slip).

And Robby—O.K. I admit that I am very proud of all my children. He is so very special—that funny sense of humor. This year his foot is as big as mine and it is the first year in ten that he is not my baby.

We will remember this Thanksgiving as the first with Will. Unknowingly, he has brought many changes into our lives. This was the year we made our big house bigger—the year of my nine-month pregnancy that felt like two years. Nine months of worry about Will's health knowing that the love would be the same regardless. Every day I kiss him with wistfulness—remembering his brothers and sister who only yesterday were his size and knowing that tomorrow he will be as big as they are. I kiss him with joy that his dad and I still love each other enough to start over with him after all these years. I kiss him with love that he is himself, beautiful and unique. I kiss him with thankfulness that he was born so perfect from such an old egg.

Yes, this is a day of Thanksgiving for sixteen wonderful years that get better and better. I know that I could never be deserving of these many blessings, but I pray that I will always be appreciative.

* * * *

Are You Sure This Is Mine?

Usually, when Rob and I fill stockings on Christmas eve, we joke about which one of us is more tired, or we laugh at the funny, obvious shapes of the stockings we fill for each other. This year I cry. We stand here with a new stocking to fill for Will while Jay's mom in the house behind us has an old stocking with no one to fill it for.

* * * *

When D.J. had puppies, John wanted Beth to have her pick. Beth chose Millie, but for some reason Millie chose Chris as her master. We often said she wasn't very bright, the way she confused carpet for grass. She ate a stick of butter once and left paw prints on the table as evidence. Once she ate a K Mart sack to get at the bag of chocolate chips inside and she often stood in the middle of the street watching cars.

Somehow, she knew when her favorite day came—Sunday. There isn't much traffic early Sunday when a fifteen-year-old delivers papers, so that was the only day Chris let her run his paper route with him. She circled every yard jumping at his overstuffed bag.

On this dark and rainy Friday morning I have to tell the boy who never cries that Millie's lifeless body was found on the street. Then I leave him in his

Judy Gill Milford

room, alone with his tears while I pretend not to know that he would not cry for me.

* * * *

Grenada Crisis—Viewed by Middle-class Mom

After the civil defense drills,
fallout shelter constructions,
and nuclear war movies
of my teenage years,
Followed by Vietnam which
threatened classmates and friends,
I settled into a peaceful era
as a young bride with willing
confidence in the future.
Suddenly, I am almost forty with teen-age sons.
I've tried to teach the boys to be
honest, trusting, compassionate young men.
The day's blissful jumble of swim, guitar and
　　tennis lessons, scouting, Little League
is shattered by the Channel 6 New Bulletin.
It never occurred to me
that I should teach them how
To fight.

* * * *

Are You Sure This Is Mine?

Faded Lines

I have never wished to be a child again
or tried to leave responsibility behind.
But sometimes, like today,
when every hour is clouded
I remember days
when answers were easy
  black—white
  wrong—right.
In the shadows of today
when the fairness of the ball
depends on where one stands
in relation to the line,
how reassuring it would be
to have some authority figure
make a decision
and know that it was right,
really right,
Just because he said so.

* * * *

Part Three

Wait a Minute, God

VII

Then he said, "I tell you solemnly, unless you change and become like little children you will never enter the kingdom of heaven. And so, the one who makes himself as little as this little child is the greatest in the kingdom of heaven." (Matthew 18:3)

GOD, wait a minute. I think you made a mistake. I've already had one crisis of faith. And it was a good one—lasted several years. I don't think I'm scheduled for another. Are you sure this doesn't belong to someone else?

* * * *

I wish that I still had
the pure, clean, unquestioning
faith of a child.
I remember that faith;
   the one that did not question—if.
How did I get from then to now?

Judy Gill Milford

I know that there is no return
for growth has taken all the innocence
which kept that faith alive.
I loathe the darker side of me
which lets the doubts creep in,
but still they come.
I want to love, to trust, have faith
To become like a child
Again.

* * * *

Why couldn't I stay in that wonderful period forever—the one right after God renewed my faith? Believing was a relief after non-belief. I could have basked in that spot forever trusting in him.

To teach me humility
God has stripped me bare.
I stand before him now
with nothing—
but my very soul.
I am weak where once I thought
was strength.
What pain that knowledge brings.
I stand before him small and undefined,
as one who never knew him
and I am ashamed.
How can he love me
as I am?

Are You Sure This Is Mine?

I was so quick to judge others,
so eager to believe in me.

* * * *

Reading Thomas a Kempis' *Imitation of Christ* I almost feel that he wrote it for me. Every chapter contains an important lesson. One that I have difficulty learning.

* * * *

One of the worst things that happened back there in the garden of Eden was that Adam and Eve decided that they had to cover up their nakedness. That was the beginning of deceit, pretense and "keeping up with the Jones." Most of our "things" are not required to meet our needs. They are just part of a constant scramble of individuals in search of a fancier fig leaf—frills to keep the inner person from being revealed.

* * * *

Beth, Chris and Robby are constant reminders that that before we know it Will, too, will be grown. Different mothering thoughts go through my head than when they were small.

Judy Gill Milford

Responsibility*

If I could always be there
To catch you when you fall,
I wouldn't have to tell you "no"
Or teach you much at all.
We'd spend each day in laughter.
We'd have a lot of fun.
Each hour would be adventure
For this mother and her son.
But quickly you are changing
In the things you do and say.
We cannot live forever
Involved in children's play.
Each day I'm growing older,
So I'll teach you all I can.
I will always be your mother,
But someday you must be a man.

*Realizations on becoming a mother—again, at 38

* * * *

God, grant me time to enjoy the waterfall, but not too much time. I must not live until the waterfall has lost its wonder for me.

God, grant me the time to see my grandchildren, but not too much time. I must not last so long that my grandchildren cannot see me as a person.

* * * *

Are You Sure This Is Mine?

I have just this moment realized that I strive more to be like Paul than Christ. In my struggle for growth in Christ through study of Paul's letters, I have come to know Paul well. I admire him and find myself trying to imitate him. Perhaps, because Paul is totally man, his qualities seem more attainable to me than those of Jesus Christ-God who came as man.

* * * *

People often pose the hypothetical question, "If your house was burning, and you could only save one thing, what would you save?"

We were gone only an hour-and-a-half to get a sandwich Sunday night. When we got back, smoke was so thick we could not go into the house even to telephone. Firemen had trouble finding the source of the problem. After checking the heating system and kitchen, they found the fire in Robby's room.

Later, after the firemen were gone and the fire was safely out, I realized that not once did I think about trying to get to photographs, papers or any of the things I thought I was attached to. The one thought, ever present and foremost, was the safety of the firemen and family members. I knew that if anyone was injured putting out the fire, I would never get over it.

* * * *

Judy Gill Milford

Strangers have invaded our home. A cleaning service goes into every room emptying private drawers and wiping smoke from our most personal possessions. In embarrassment I scoop up an assortment of feminine articles from my bathroom vanity drawer and dump them into the trash saying, "Oh, these old things," before he has a chance to go over them piece by piece. I feel almost as if my inner life has been violated. Under the scrutiny of outsiders I wonder why we kept many things which were of value before.

* * * *

Strangely, many things are easy to throw away now. A weight of responsibility is lifted. I am no longer accountable for everything that has passed through these doors. I can now say, "Oh, I lost that in the fire." Small consolation for this mess—this chaos that fills our lives.

Each day is filled with cleaning and shopping for replacements for things that burned in Robby's room. I choose new wallpaper to replace discontinued patterns which were smoked. I have reached the point where I am ready to accept any loss. I am sick of shopping and making choices. I wash load after load of smoked clothes and linens. Not even outgrown children's clothing stored in boxes escaped the grey monster. We have a new landmark on the

Are You Sure This Is Mine?

time-line of our lives. Everything happened before or after the fire.

* * * *

I don't recall ever reading or hearing the Bible story of Abraham and Isaac as a child without being angry either at Abraham for being willing to sacrifice his son or at God for asking him to. It took me years to understand. Oh, I knew that we were supposed to love God above all things, but that did little to alleviate the pain I felt for Isaac when he realized what his dad was going to do to him. My motherhood at twenty-three did nothing to change my indignance, for I knew I would give my life or go through any amount of suffering for any one of my children. Didn't Abraham experience these same protective feelings for Isaac? If he did, surely his love for and trust in God must put my feeble devotion to God to shame. My ultimate understanding came at last one day in meditating on God as the father of Jesus. If Abraham (as mankind) had not loved God enough to give his son as a sacrifice, would God have still deemed us worth saving through the sacrifice of *his* only son?

* * * *

Many times when I was younger I would look at the examples of Peter, David, Paul and all those im-

Judy Gill Milford

perfect others in the Bible and wonder why we didn't have perfect examples to pattern ourselves after. I have learned many things since then from all of them. Peter was brave and strong during Jesus' arrest. He stood up to the soldiers, cut off the ear. But then, Jesus did not allow him to fight. "Jesus said to Peter, 'Put your sword back in its scabbard; am I not to drink the cup that the Father has given me?'" (John 18:11). After that, Peter's strength failed. He denied Jesus just as Jesus had predicted. I am a lot like Peter. I thought I knew what God's call was for me. I felt strong. When I learned my call was not as I had anticipated, I found a weakness I didn't know existed. Why did I not know better than to second-guess the plan of God? It is encouraging to know that others like Peter had problems with weakness. Peter failed God, but God's call to him was the same. I am thankful for that.

* * * *

Thoreau once said, "In winter, even man is to a slight extent dormant, just as some animals are but partially awake though not commonly classed with those that hibernate."

I can understand why he made that observation. I hate the winter rainy season when sunshine is scarce and the earth sloppy.

> Why does darkness
> bring such gloom

Are You Sure This Is Mine?

penetrating every room,
while the light brings sweet release,
harmony, and inner peace?

* * * *

When we talk, you and I, don't heap up empty words—what the young people call "B.S." Don't rob me of the chance to learn from your experiences, to change because I see the way you feel.

If you give me less than honesty, you did not think that I could measure up, meet the challenge of dealing with the truth. Because of that I miss a chance to grow that may not come again. Trust me enough to give me your truth, and I will weigh each word for fairness, measure my thoughts by your remarks and perhaps move a little closer to the place where you stand.

* * * *

Every Thursday while Will is at Mother's Day Out, I stop at the Christian book store next to St. Francis De Sales. The owner has many paperback copies of books I have wanted for a long time. I buy only one or two at a time. I have *New Seeds of Contemplation, The New Man,* and *Love and Living* by Thomas Merton. I also got *Imitation of Christ* by Thomas a Kempis, *Interior Castle* by St. Teresa of Avila, and *Dark Night of the Soul* by St. John of the Cross. *My Other Self* by Charles Enzler is sort of a modern *Imitation of*

Christ. I even found *Confessions of St. Augustine.* It is a different translation than the one at the library but that doesn't matter. I haven't finished reading all of them. If only my mind would contain all that I try to put in it. I surround myself with my favorites hoping to learn everything, but every time I pick up one of the books to read, I see something that is completely new.

* * * *

Will talks more than the other three did at his age. He talks *all* the time. Maybe it's just that they talked to each other some and he talks mostly to me, but at night when he goes to sleep, I am exhausted from answering questions. I wouldn't want him to stop asking, but it looks as if his life will be filled with as many questions as mine.

Conversations with Will

Will: Did God make J.J.?
Mom: Yes.
Will: But her not go to church.
Mom: Well, most people go to church to talk to God and thank him but dogs and other animals cannot talk or think so it would not do any good for them to go.
Will: She could pray with her paws.
Will: Who was the first family?
Mom: What do you mean?

Will: Who were the first people in the house when the dinosaurs were disappearing?

Will (on the way to church for directory photos): Mom, do you see people when you die?
Mom: I don't know, Will.
Will: Tell me yes or no.
Mom: Yes, I think you do because if you are in heaven with God, you see him and the people there.
Will: Is it light or dark, when you die?
Mom: I don't know.
Will: Tell me yes or no.
Mom: Light, I think.
Will: I hope it is dark. Will we be inside or outside?
Mom: When?
Will: When we have our pictures taken for the directory?

Will: Did we always live in this house?
Mom: We've lived here a long time.
Will: Will we always live here?
Mom: I don't know. We are not planning to move.
Will: Where did we live before we lived here?
Mom: Well, when Chris was your age, we lived in Memphis. Beth, Chris, Robby, Dad and I lived there before you were born.
Will: Where did I live when you lived in Memphis?
Mom: Nowhere. You were not born yet.
Will: Did J.J. live in Memphis with you?
Mom: Yes.

Judy Gill Milford

Will: Oh, I wanted her to live here with me.
Mom: But you didn't live here when we lived in Memphis. That was before you were born.
Will: Well, where did I live before I was born—nowhere?
Mom: You were an idea that God had.
Will: Oh, was that before God made me?

Will: Mom, what do yellow things taste like?
Mom: What do you think?
Will: Color, I think they taste like color.

Will: Who was I before I was a little boy?
   What is in me?
   Mom, where was I when you didn't have me?
   I have two kinds of thinking—thinking in my mouth and thinking in my thoughts.

* * * *

Our family grows—is almost grown. We sit here with our many presents under the tree and I feel guilt as well as pride. The pride is easy to explain for it is pride in each of you as the persons you have become and are becoming. The guilt—well, the guilt arises because we have so much while others have little. What right do we have to be so happy when others are not?

* * * *

Are You Sure This Is Mine?

If we had not had Will when Beth, Chris and Robby were older I might never have realized how little they remember about their early years. What a conscientious mother I was. We played. I spent time with them. I carried Robby's stroller up and down the Pink Palace steps so that the four of us could explore the museum. We went to the zoo, took swimming lessons at the Y, went to story hours at the library, flew kites in the park. During those early years they filled my life. Now, they look at Will and say, "You never did that with me." I wonder if that huge investment I made in them was wasted time or if they benefited in ways they are not aware of.

* * * *

I don't think I can go along with the popular belief "once saved, always saved" (although I admit it does have certain appeal). If that belief were true, the devil's work would be cut in half. When a person joined the church or "got saved," the devil would just say "O.K. God, you win that one," and he'd go bother someone else. Unfortunately, that is not the way it works. The old devil keeps hounding us until the day we die, hoping to get in the last word. I know that he won't leave me alone and he knows exactly where my weaknesses lie. I fight the same battles over and over.

* * * *

Judy Gill Milford

VIII

I have the strength to face all conditions by the power that Christ gives me. (Philippians 4:13)

I DON'T know myself as well today as I did a year ago. I am not the person I thought I was. The past year has brought many changes caused by age, stress, health. Whatever the cause, they have revealed weaknesses that I did not consider part of my character. Last year I was strong and in control. Now, I see myself trying to regain control.

* * * *

I fear that I won't live long enough to do all that I want to do. There is so much to taste. I know there won't be time. I want to paint. I want to write. I want to see my children grown, married, happy. Oh God, please let them be happy. Not a happiness of having everything, but a happiness of being content with what they have, of being able to deal with their lives

Are You Sure This Is Mine?

and their problems. A happiness that comes with faith.

* * * *

I am the lowest of all creatures. I want to feel an undying, unfaltering, unfailing love for God—for Jesus. I want to know him, really know him. I read. I study, I pray (some, but not enough). I fail. I can never measure up to what I want to feel. I want to be filled to overflowing with love. Why can't I?

Why do I continuously have periods of independence when I think I can make it on my own? I have been shown again and again that alone I am nothing, alone I make myself miserable. Relying on him I can understand anything.

There have been times when I was so close to God, times when I rested totally in his care. Those were times of great peace. Why would anyone forego that peace for the torment that I now feel—the torment of not loving as I should? Perhaps, this is another lesson I must learn for this is humbling and my pride gets in my way.

* * * *

The hardest thing about where I am now is that I don't feel I'm the best I've ever been. Surely, the commercial did not lie—the one with the wonderful looking blue-eyed man who looks straight at me and says,

Judy Gill Milford

"You're not getting older, you're getting better." For years, I felt good because each day I grew.

Now, I don't feel in control of my life. I had assumed that I would continue to get better and better and better. Maybe I was in need of a humbling experience. Well, I got it.

I know I have not handled the stresses of the past few years as well as I expected. I thought I could handle anything and here I am stumbling around. Perhaps this is a period of growth to help me have more compassion for and understanding of other people.

* * * *

I know that we are supposedly all born in a state of sin because of Adam and Eve. I accept that, but I was just thinking—aren't we the same as Adam and Eve? How are we any different? There they were in the world possessing free choice. They were tempted, and chose worldliness. That is exactly what we do generation after generation. If we were to retain free choice, how is our state any different than it would have been had Eve not tasted the fruit?

* * * *

If I had to be something else, not human, I would not choose to be a vine, strong but dependent, creeping, clinging, caressing, sometimes choking that which gives it strength. I would be a tree. Sometimes, in spring, I would be a dogwood fresh and fragile,

Are You Sure This Is Mine?

gracefully dancing in the breeze. In winter I might be a tall majestic fir, a pine that shimmers in the snow, or even a birch whose bark blends against the white. In summer I would be an oak—tall, sturdy and strong. Or maybe I would be an apple, peach or pear offering juicy fruit free for the picking. An autumn tree would be the hardest tree to choose with sycamore, sweetgum, maple, oak and poplar. How could I possibly choose, for each has beauty. They compliment each other magnificently. I do know I would never be the tree that rains dry colorless leaves to the ground with the first cool wind that blows across September.

* * * *

Today my mom stopped by as she so often does when she comes to Paducah shopping. She brought several of my old dolls from her attic. All of them were special but Janie, the oldest, is my favorite. Sleeping memories were awakened when my hands enclosed her.

> The four who once were cuddly, soft and warm,
> Dependent on my nurturing and care,
> Today are self-sufficient, straight and tall
> With little need of me or time to share.
> But sitting here with molded hair worn thin,
> Cracks like road maps telling where you've been,
> Once-bright flashing eyes, now clouded dim,
> You're considered trash by all of them.

Judy Gill Milford

They would never guess that I still love you.
They don't know the memories you've fed.
For all my dreams of yesterday's tomorrows
Are locked inside your battered little head.

* * * *

After teaching first grade CCD for five years before Will was born, I did not know if I would teach again. I cared about the children, was sensitive to their needs, but I wasn't a very good teacher, maybe even boring. I certainly didn't expect to teach high school, but that age group is less formidable now that we have teenagers of our own. In this matrimony class prepared by Father Chuck Gallagher, S.J. and Joe and Judy McDonald, a couple shares their marriage with the class. Rob and I will do the preparation together, but because of his work, I will be the only one teaching. I think we have a lot of positive things to share and I am comfortable with the informal structure of the class. I could not handle a lecture where I stood over the class. I will be their equals and will learn as much from them as they from me—maybe more.

* * * *

Sometimes, it seems that the most fortunate people are those who come from poor or deprived families. I think that I benefited from having little when I was young and have seen evidence to support this idea in many others. Knowing this, why are we so intent on

Are You Sure This Is Mine?

working to provide our children with things that we never had? Are we bringing destruction to our children when, in fact, what we want most in the world is to protect them and assure their success and happiness?

* * * *

Oh God, I place my children in your hands. We have tried to give them our values. Parenting is important to us, but there are so many other influences on them in the world, forces pulling them toward worldliness and away from you. I know that it is only through your intervention that they can be happy. Only by placing their trust in you can they survive. Help them, please, to learn how important it is to put you first and to realize that *things* are only *things*.

* * * *

I suspect that the only time I can really write is when I am walking closely with God. That does not mean that my writing is particularly religious, only that my relationship with God adds the clarity, the single-mindedness to my life that allows me to focus on a single area to the degree that there is a moment of insight in which I can be creative.

* * * *

I am going through one of the most difficult times of my entire life. My problems are not even my own.

Judy Gill Milford

No one could have told me that parenting would be like this. How is it that we feel our children's pain so distinctly?

* * * *

I wish I could be assured that our children would take our advice about relationships with the opposite sex. Premarital sex is common among teenagers. Why is this practice accepted? Many people say teens are different. How different are they? Are hormones in existence today that were non-existent thirty years ago? Does the blood run hotter in their veins than it did in ours? Is there scientific evidence to suggest that the passion they feel is more intense than ours was? If the answer to these questions is "No," it is not the teens that are different, it is the society that is telling them it is all right to give in to every passion—the society that encourages free sex through TV, movies, music and magazines. Increase in sexually transmitted diseases alone should tell us that there are more reasons for abstaining than for giving in. I know I am sounding like a prude, but I have seen evidence through the years that denying oneself for a good cause builds character, while giving in to every passion makes us weak. Let's give them a little encouragement to be patient, to be strong—instead of just saying, "Oh well, things are different now." I am certainly glad that my parents didn't take that attitude. I would probably have gotten myself into a heap of trouble.

Part Four

Wally and Me

IX

For we fix our attention, not on things that are seen, but on things that are unseen. What can be seen lasts only for a time, but what cannot be seen lasts forever. (II Corinthians 4:18)[1]

AS A four-year-old, Will is completely at the mercy of cereal advertising gimmicks. In spite of my nutrition-teaching efforts, he expectantly chooses the box with the most exciting offer on the lower right corner. For a while he thought that everything pictured in that corner was actually in the box. After two or three disappointments he learned to ask if the item pictured was in the box or had to be ordered with money and box tops.

Later he learned that the special prize rarely, if ever, measures up to its image and his expectations. Wally, the glow-in-the-dark wall-walker was the best cereal box prize we ever got. After we rescued Wally from beneath the cereal and freed him from the cellophane, we took him into the hall bathroom (we needed complete darkness). We stuck Wally as high

Judy Gill Milford

as possible on the wall and watched him walk down over and over using different positions on each wall. But that wasn't all. With our eyes on Wally, we could walk all over the room in the dark without stumbling or getting lost. In that black room with Wally and Will, I realized that walking in the dark with Wally is a lot like walking in the world with God. If we keep our eyes fixed on God, we are all right but when we take our eyes off him to look around at other things in the world, we are apt to stumble and fall.

* * * *

Why are there so many disposables today? Nothing is intended to last. Use it and throw it away. We go from small items like contact lenses and razors which do not create much litter to larger things like diapers and fast food containers which are an increasing problem.

Our clothes are intended to be worn one or two seasons. Fashion industry dictates that they be replaced by changing hemlines, lapels, pant leg widths, acceptable color-coordinates. Anything to make sure that last year's clothes look dated. Older homes and buildings are abandoned for new ones. Old cars cover the countryside. I once passed a place in the east where old cars were lined up as far as I could see in every direction. I got away from there as quickly as I could.

The most disturbing product of our disposable

Are You Sure This Is Mine?

society is people. Aren't many abortions performed as a convenience? The mother-to-be isn't ready for the responsibility so the baby becomes disposable. Relationships are not nurtured or valued. People are used and discarded as never before. A relationship is good as long as it is convenient. When it becomes a problem, it is not considered worth saving. Is it that much easier to start a new one?

* * * *

Our friendship with Jim and Gail is unique. Other friendships come and go. This one remains constant. We are separated by miles, but through every change in our lives, the bond has remained unbroken, unstrained. It is comforting in these times for a treasure such as this to exist.

* * * *

At the paperback book store I found another book by Madeleine L'Engle, *Walking on Water,* about the relationship between art and Christianity. I have never known anyone whose outlook seemed as much like my own. I think about writing her a letter. That sounds silly. I have never even thought of communicating with a famous person before. I read her pages and I am with a friend whom I will never meet.

* * * *

Judy Gill Milford

There is something wrong in my life. I made it through the hectic pre-Christmas preparations by holding on to the thought that after Christmas I would have time. Well, after-Christmas is here and I still don't have time. These little jobs that have to be done—the ones that give no sense of satisfaction, no feeling of productivity—are draining me. I hate emptying waste baskets every day—no one could make that much trash. I hate picking up dirty laundry—more clothing than six people could possibly wear. I wouldn't mind if it was a reasonable amount, or if it stayed done for a day or two, but the same trash, the same dirty laundry, even the same food-covered dishes day after day, year after year. It is intolerable!

* * * *

Sometimes, my life is
a spool of thread
neatly wound
one continuous flowing strand
Other times the spool
is covered with loose ends
raveling in frightening disarray
I look for a piece long enough
to work with
There is none

* * * *

Are You Sure This Is Mine?

I try to imagine what it would have been like living in Jesus' day. Knowing myself as I do, how would I have viewed him? Would I have suspected him of being a religious fanatic—crazy? Would I have recognized him as Savior, or completely ignored him? Would I have had the courage to walk with him? Would I have kept very silent when the situation got dangerous from fear of endangering my family? I would like to think that I would believe, love and stand firm, but I have never done anything terribly courageous and I wonder....

* * * *

In John 17:12 we are told, "While I was with them, I kept those you had given me true to your name. I have watched over them and not one is lost except the one who chose to be lost, and this was to fulfill the scriptures." Did Judas have a choice? If God and Jesus both knew what would happen and who would betray Jesus, was it pre-ordained and did he ever have a chance? If God knows what I will do, in one sense it seems that it is beyond my power to control and make choices, but I guess that he knows my nature so well that he knows perfectly every choice that I will make better than I myself know.

* * * *

Judy Gill Milford

If Jesus had lived in our convenience-oriented society, would he see us as worthy of his journey to the cross or would it have been too inconvenient?

* * * *

We as parents need to remember that we do not embrace all the ideas and beliefs of our friends, if we are to deal with our children effectively. I remember one time that I noticed an undesirable trait in one of Beth's friends. When I pointed this flaw out to Beth, she became defensive. This disturbed me. I had wrongly assumed that since my daughter chose her friend, Beth must agree with her about everything.

Wouldn't I be offended if Beth or anyone else judged me by my friends? I respect them, but I respect myself more. I stand apart from them. I view their weaknesses objectively and accept them as they are. I must trust Beth and the boys enough to know that they can make the same discernments.

As parents, it is normal for us to be concerned that a child might be influenced by a friend, but we also need to give our children enough credit to believe that they will make responsible choices. They could be a positive influence on their friends.

* * * *

After almost nineteen years of parenting I am still surprised by the degree to which we hurt for our

Are You Sure This Is Mine?

children. It is fairly easy to sympathize with others, but when the other person is your own child, the pain is much more intense. Whether the source of pain is a cut finger, broken leg, the disappointment of a lost soccer game or a jilting lover, the pain could not be more real if you stubbed your own toe unexpectedly in the dark.

* * * *

For a long time after my recommitment to God, I was anxious to know what his plan was for me. I felt that since he called me back to him when I was relatively young, he must have a big mission for me to accomplish. Either that or I was just about finished (as in dead) and he wanted me to get straightened out and on the right track before I died.

I still feel that he has a plan for me but I also now know that I am such a slow learner about some things that he knew it was going to take me a *long* time to find the answers and the sooner I got started, the better.

* * * *

Being raised a Methodist, I've never found it easy to pray the Rosary as many long-time Catholics do. When I was growing up we always went straight to God. That route is still most natural for me. In recent years with the children growing older, I worry about

Judy Gill Milford

them more and more. Knowing that we have done all we can to instill in them the values we feel are important, I have turned increasingly to prayer for them. Sometimes, during a walk or a long drive, I offer these prayers for each of the four children with the feeling that if I lift them up to God he will hold them a little more tenderly.

* * * *

Recently, I read a book, *The God Who Is There* by Francis A. Schaeffer which criticized Soren Kierkegaard, saying that he was both the father of the new theological thinking and of modern secular thinking.

I have only one book by Kierkegaard, *Purity of Heart Is to Will One Thing*. I rather like it. I underlined almost half the book (the highest compliment I pay is to underline so that I can find the good parts easily when I reread).

* * * *

All that we know of God is that which he has chosen to reveal to us. It is possible and even probable that there is much that we will never know about him. He would not reveal to us something outside of the realm of human understanding for it would be of no use to us.

* * * *

Are You Sure This Is Mine?

X

. . . Now it is impossible to please God without faith, since anyone who comes to him must believe that he exists and rewards those who try to find him. (Hebrews 11:6)

OH GOD, I believe that you exist. I am trying so hard to find you. I seek your face. Why is it so hard to find?

Once I was so broken by fear that I was near despair. God called me back to him. I was healed, made new, renewed. Why, having experienced this, would I ever allow myself to be entangled in the world again? Yet, here I am struggling once again. Why, oh why do we make the same mistakes over and over?

* * * *

Once again in Thomas a Kempis' *Imitation of Christ* I find words written for me. "When you have the spirit of fervor, think how you will act when the

Judy Gill Milford

fervor is past; when it is past, think that the fervor, which to My honor and for your testing I have withdrawn for a time, may soon come to you again."[1] That is one thing that is bothering me—the memory of the fervor that I no longer feel.

In Thomas Green's *When the Well Runs Dry*, I find that "as we grow we may well feel we are slipping farther from God, not because we are regressing but because we are becoming more aware of who we really are. The closer we come to the light of God, the darker our own darkness appears by contrast."[2] Those are encouraging words. I want to believe them but I don't see how I could be closer to God when I feel so much darker than I did before. I want to feel what I see in Psalm 73:25,26 "I look to no one else in heaven, I delight in nothing else on earth. My flesh and my heart are pining with love, my heart's Rock, my own, God forever!"

* * * *

I have always known that I was different. I never really fit. While others ran and played, rode their bikes and yelled in wreckless glee, I thought a lot, observed, existed inside myself and longed to be a part of the cheerful crowd that never gave a thought to the outcome of any action—or tomorrow. Throughout high school and college I tried to play the game. The "in" crowd looked so happy. I was always just outside the outer rim, looking in, sometimes reach-

Are You Sure This Is Mine?

ing in, and finally after a few years of marriage, belonging. I learned to play the game well. Now, I find that part of me must move back within myself. Not everyone can live that carefree life.

* * * *

I just got back from the Kentucky State Poetry Society's annual meeting in Bardstown. What a wonderful experience! Now I know what I have always been. Why did it take me so long to find out? I love Rob more right now than ever before. He can let me go away for a weekend without any attempt to make me feel guilty for leaving the children and house to him. He shows no sign of jealousy. That exhibits such confidence. Many men could learn from him.

* * * *

We are different, he and I—
Always have been. Suits me.
He fills up the part of me
That I am not.
Together we make a whole.
But what if . . .
if I was less than I could
or should be—
if I were less than half
and he was, too,

Judy Gill Milford

would it take more than
two people to make a whole?

Is that what happens to couples sometimes—one of them goes off in search of the rest of themselves?

* * * *

There are some people that I see about town who refuse to grow up. Some writers have referred to this condition as the "Peter Pan Syndrome." I remember that song, "I won't grow up, I don't want to go to school." It was entertaining when Peter Pan sang it. Not quite as entertaining when we observe the same behavior in forty-five and fifty-year-old men. Don't we all have areas of childhood that we hang on to stubbornly? That could explain why a forty-five-year-old woman would watch squirrels playing in the yard instead of cleaning window sills, how she could sit in a gravel pile looking for special rocks, or why she would want to climb the neighbor's tree to feel the texture of the upper branches. In my mind I know that the Peter Pans are as scornful of me as I am of them. I guess some of our childish diversions are more harmless than others.

* * * *

One of the poets I met at Bardstown wrote about his experiences in Vietnam. I cannot get his words from my mind. I have to write.

Are You Sure This Is Mine?

In '66 when we married,
the army was calling young men to serve,
  young men who were single.
In '67 when we started our family,
  they were calling young men
  who were married;
  married but childless.
In the years that followed,
when we thought about the war,
we never felt guilty, never looked back.
After all, we played by the rules,
  didn't march to protest the war
    that no one wanted
  didn't burn draft cards
  didn't run to Canada
  didn't pull any dirty tricks to stay home.
But yesterday, in '86 when I read
one soldier's pain
still burning after twenty years
and he asked if I was there, in Nam
I couldn't look into his eyes.

* * * *

I spent the first thirty-five years watching, listening, observing. I hope to spend the next thirty-five or so sorting and recording my reactions and conclusions to the first thirty-five.

* * * *

Judy Gill Milford

My brain is full of dodge-em cars that have been running independently on tracks for years, never making contact. Now, they are beginning to break away, to bump instead of dodge and each point of impact represents a moment of insight—creativity.

* * * *

> Sometimes, it is harder
> than other times
> to maintain the balance
> between me
> and us.

* * * *

Kim told me about her involvement with a group called Mother-to-Mother. It is part of the Paducah Co-operative Ministry and pairs adequate income mothers with inadequate income mothers for special friendship. The mothers learn from and support each other.

* * * *

My new MTM friend is Brooke. Before I met her I didn't know what we would say to each other, but I feel that we have been friends for a long time. We are a lot alike because we both have teenagers and a preschooler. It is challenging to jump back and forth between the problems of those two age groups so we

Are You Sure This Is Mine?

have a lot to share in that one area alone. Whichever age I am dealing with at the moment seems the worst. I wish that some of my friends and their husbands could see how hard some of these young women work to make positive changes in their lives.

* * * *

It is exciting to watch the world of a baby expand. In the beginning, everything revolves about his needs. Gradually, he reaches out taking in more and more, encompassing family, friends, classmates, community and the world as he becomes an adult. Now, during my dad's hospitalization, I see the not-so-exciting part of the process. Since he has been in Intensive Care, I have seen his world shrink until all that remains is the meeting of his most basic needs. All of his energy is used surviving. It is painful to watch him withering into himself, to search his face for a spark of vitality, to find none.

* * * *

Good has come from my dad's illness. Sitting at the hospital waiting and watching our lives centered on his recovery, our family has grown closer. We are reacquainted. We play silly games in the IC waiting room to pass time and keep each other encouraged. We become friends as never before.

* * * *

Judy Gill Milford

Our watching, waiting and praying has been rewarded. He has been moved from ICU to a room and we see signs that he is returning.

* * * *

I just received word that one of the poets that I met in Bardstown is dead. I shook his hand, bought his book and now I find that he has taken his own life. How could he do that? I reread his poems for clues but find none. Was he unable to maintain the balance?

Many people, if they suddenly came upon God, holding the pain of mankind pulsing in the palm of his hand, would turn their back and walk away from it, cover it with something to make it invisible, knock it off with disgust and kick or roll it under the bed—anything to pretend that it doesn't exist.

The writer must look at it, approach it, walk around it, roll it over, view it from every possible angle, pick it up, palpate, poke, prod and, if possible, even crawl inside it.

Having explored, examined, experienced the intensity, sometimes, she cannot live with the awful truth.

* * * *

Are You Sure This Is Mine?

Not believing in God and knowing that there is a God is like the difference between being in a big house alone after dark, and being in the house with your parents in the other room. When your parents are there you don't really know what they would do if there was a problem, but you feel safe, secure and warm knowing they are there.

If I think about the possibility of God not being real, the entire world reverts to chaos. It is no wonder there is so much hopelessness in the world. Without God as the master planner this place is a mess with no chance for survival. Sort of like a house being built without a blueprint, or a cake without a recipe.

* * * *

I remember when a person who studied the Bible and prayed was a good Christian or perhaps if he went to Mass every day and prayed the Rosary a lot he was a devout Catholic. Now a person who fits that description is likely to be referred to as a religious fanatic or a "Bible-thumping weirdo."

Publicity about several famous evangelists has done more to tarnish the image of the Christian recently than any anti-Christian could have hoped for.

Also, when was the last time you saw a Christian portrayed favorably on TV? They are always fanatics, serial killers or pathetic creatures worth a few

Judy Gill Milford

laughs. Our children are being brain-washed and they don't even know it. What can be done?

* * * *

If someone could solve a few of the little everyday annoyances my life would be simpler and I could focus on bigger problems. Here are some that you might work on:

1. *Junk Mail.* Last week we received an orange grove catalog, two department store catalogs, a library overdue notice (from son's university), a department store make-up ad, an IMPORTANT NOTICE for winning fantastic prizes in a marketing contest, a notification of selection as finalist in national promotion contest, a request for a donation to a monastery, and opportunities to contribute to four separate organizations for preserving and conserving various aspects of our environment.

I want to save our wildlands, protect natural resources, slow the "greenhouse effect," stop cutting and burning of rain forests but let's face it, I can't do it all. I even got an invitation from the NRA (I hate guns) and a pro-life and a pro-choice publication in the same mail. There should be a law against placing a person's name on a list unless she requested it there.

2. *Gender changes.* I've always known that sometimes "man" is sexless, meaning mankind, everyone, everywhere, humans. I have never had a problem

Are You Sure This Is Mine?

with that until someone started making all of these gender changes. How can I go to church and be prayerful and worshipful when somebody keeps changing the words to the songs. Instead of walking with my brother (which to me meant walking with everyone, black, white, young, old, fat, thin) I am walking with my neighbor. I find these gender changes distracting and petty.

3. *Hair in bathrooms.* Mothers of hairless families are especially blessed by God. They spend less time cleaning. When I was a little girl, my parents told me people have hair on different parts of their bodies for protection dating back to the times when people wore little clothing and lived outside or in caves. I don't believe it. Cleaning our families' hair from the bathroom is another punishment from God for what Eve did to Adam in the garden.

4. *Public restroom doors.* Can't someone make those locks line up with the part on the other side?

5. *Game boxes.* We have stacks of games. Monopoly, Clue, Stratego, Careers, Payday, etc. After repeated tapings, the corners are still flat. Scrabble alone stands up, probably because no one will play with me. What the world needs is a better game box.

* * * *

I still remember one of the few arguments that my mom and dad had when I was a teenager. I was so surprised to hear Mom say to Dad, "You just think

Judy Gill Milford

you are so perfect." I asked her about that later. As far as I could see that couldn't be farther from the truth. She admitted to me that it wasn't Dad who thought he was perfect. She did. It made her mad, and perhaps a little scared because he was so often right. She wanted to be sure that he knew he made mistakes lest he cast her aside as unworthy of him. When I feel weak, I must find weakness in others. When I am frustrated about my inability to keep the house clean and neat, I am likely to criticize Rob for throwing everything away or for putting things away in a disorganized manner. Do I feel that I must remind him that he is imperfect to balance my imperfection? I think that is the nature of we humans. The less secure we are about ourselves, the more important it is that we find flaws in others. Those who criticize others the most inwardly feel that they themselves deserve criticism. They are merely trying to achieve a balance.

* * * *

It is bad enough to get old, to feel the same inside and have everyone looking at an old person, but to cease to exist . . . that is death. Death is something that my mind tries to comprehend but refuses to accept.

* * * *

Are You Sure This Is Mine?

Will my death be a silent slipping away in the darkness of a lonely room, or will there be a band to play my life in wild explosive lights with no encores?

* * * *

Proclamation of 1986

Whereas, on the twenty-fifth of December, in the year of our Lord one thousand nine hundred and eighty-six, a proclamation was issued by the mother of the Milford household containing the following:

Whereas the older Milford sons, Christopher and Robb, decided in their early pre-teen years that it was no longer proper to hug or be hugged by the mother or father of the family, and whereas the Milford mother being of natural reserve, a person not given to spontaneous outbursts of emotion, and not wanting said Milford children to feel said mother was overprotective, over-gushy, overly-demonstrative or over-anything, said mother fell readily into the pattern of not hugging. Hugging ceased, even hugging of Elizabeth, oldest and only Milford daughter.

From then on there were no bedtime hugs, no birthday hugs, no good-by hugs, no welcome-home hugs, no Christmas hugs, no hugs of pride, no "hey, you look sad and need a lift" hugs. The Milford house was basically a "hugless house." And no matter how much the Milford mother and the Milford father loved the Milford children, and were proud of

Judy Gill Milford

the Milford children, not wishing to hug a reluctant "huggee," they did not hug.

The only Milford to hug and receive hugs freely and willingly remained youngest son William who unencumbered by learned inhibitions knew that hugs made him feel better, and was honest enough to ask for hugs from one and all.

And whereas, on this twenty-fifth day of December, the Milford mother, knowing that hugs from the Milford father and the Milford youngest son give her strength and encouragement in times of stress and fatigue, wishes that same encouragement might be imparted to older Milford children at times when it might seem fitting. The Milford mother feels the Milford children were hasty in their decision to give up the hug, and that due to their youth and inexperience at the time of said decision this choice not be deemed binding.

Therefore, I, the Milford mother, by the power invested in me as assistant to commander-in-chief of Milford household do publicly proclaim that the year of our Lord, one thousand nine hundred and eighty-seven is to be known as the "year of the hug" with the hug being reinstated in Milford household as proper, and accepted method of expressing affection with no person herein too young, too old or too macho to receive said hug whenever it might seem fitting or even desired.

* * * *

Part Five

From Sleighrides and Snowmen to Hazardous Highways

XI

The trials that you have had to bear are no more than people normally have. You can trust God not to let you be tried beyond your strength and with any trial he will give you a way out of it and the strength to bear it. (I Corinthians 10:13)

AS A pre-teen and early teenager I was intrigued by boys who were a bit rowdy, the ones who weren't afraid to use a few bad words in mysterious ways. If I had not been determined to graduate from college before marriage, I might have married too soon and been stuck with a real scoundrel. Of course, I was so square (common term in sixties, no longer used) none of those boys would have proposed anyway. As one young man so persuasively put it, "You wouldn't buy a coat without trying it on, would you?" I knew if I spent much time with him I was in for trouble.

As a young girl I secretly wanted to be just a little naughty but didn't have the courage. Now, I have the courage but too much good judgment and no desire.

Judy Gill Milford

There are a few harmless daring things I wish I had done—like joining the Peace Corps. I think middle age causes us to start thinking about those things.

* * * *

Yesterday
clean cold flakes
fell on eagerly outstretched tongues
formed fluffy white blankets
rolled into jaunty fat snowmen
encouraged exhilarating flights
down powdered, padded hills.
Today
snow promises
icy windshields
back-weary driveway shoveling
slippery hazardous highways
racks of sloshy mittens
muddy slushprints on carpeted stairs
empty marshmallowed mugs making
sloppy cocoa rings.
I wonder when I began to grow old.

* * * *

It is funny how our priorities change. Once I just wanted to live, no matter how. Then during the years that I was painting, I feared that I would lose my sight and my ability to distinguish shade, color and perception. Now that I am writing, I panic when I realize

Are You Sure This Is Mine?

that my body could live beyond my mind. What could possibly be worse than that?

* * * *

Thomas Merton makes an important observation following the illness of his father.

> Indeed, the truth that many people never understand until it is too late, is that the more you try to avoid suffering, the more you suffer, because smaller and more insignificant things begin to torture you in proportion to your fear of being hurt. The one who does most to avoid suffering is, in the end, the one who suffers most; and his suffering comes to him from things so little and trivial that one can say that it is no longer objective at all. It is his own existence, his own being that is at once the subject and the source of his pain, and his very existence and consciousness is his greatest torture. This is another of the great perversions by which the devil uses our philosophers to turn our whole nature inside out, and eviscerate all our capacities for good turning them against ourselves.[1]

* * * *

The despair that I felt a few months ago is gone. I have pulled myself back together. I had to relax and

Judy Gill Milford

slow my mind down. I am, once again, still getting better. I will be all right.

* * * *

As part of the catechetical study I am attending, we are supposed to keep a prayer journal. This is something I have never done before, but should do all the time. Excerpts from prayer journal:

Genesis 1:20-2:4

God said, "Let the waters teem with living creatures, and let birds fly above the earth within the vault of heaven." And so it was. God created great sea serpents and every kind of living creature with which the waters teem, and every kind of winged creature. God saw that it was good. God blessed them, saying, "Be fruitful, multiply, and fill the waters of the seas; and let the birds multiply upon the earth. Evening came and morning came: the fifth day.

God said, "Let the earth produce every kind of living creature: cattle, reptiles, and every kind of wild beast." And so it was. God made every kind of wild beast, every kind of cattle, and every kind of land reptile. God saw that it was good.

God said, "Let us make man in our own image, in the likeness of ourselves, and let them be masters of the fish of the sea, the birds of heaven, the cattle, all the wild beasts and all the reptiles that crawl upon the earth."

Are You Sure This Is Mine?

God created man in the image of himself,
in the image of God he created him,
male and female he created them.

God blessed them, saying to them, "Be fruitful, multiply, fill the earth and conquer it. Be masters of the fish of the sea, the birds of heaven and all living animals of the earth." God said, "See, I give you all the seed-bearing plants that are upon the whole earth, and all the trees with seed-bearing plants that are upon the whole earth, and all the trees with seed-bearing fruit; this shall be your food. To all wild beasts, all birds of heaven and all living reptiles on the earth I give all the foliage of plants for food." And so it was. God saw all he had made, and indeed it was very good. Evening came and morning came; the sixth day. Thus heaven and earth were completed with all their array. On the seventh day God completed the work he had been doing. He rested on the seventh day after all the work he had been doing.

Mark 7:1-13.

The Pharisees and some of the scribes who had come from Jerusalem gathered around him, and they noticed that some of his disciples were eating with unclean hands, that is, without washing them. For the Pharisees, and the Jews in general follow the tradition of the elders and never eat without washing their arms as far as the elbow; and on returning from the market place they never eat without first sprinkling themselves. There are also many other

Judy Gill Milford

observances which have been handed down to them concerning the washing of cups and pots and bronze dishes. So these Pharisees and scribes asked him, "Why do your disciples not respect the tradition of the elders but eat their food with unclean hands?" He answered, "It was of you hypocrites that Isaiah so rightly prophesied in the passage of scripture:

> This people honors me only with lip-service
> while their hearts are far from me.
> The worship they offer me is worthless.
> The doctrines they teach are only human
>   regulations.

You put aside the commandment of God to cling to human traditions." And he said to them, "How ingeniously you get around the commandment of God in order to preserve your own traditions! For Moses said: Do your duty to your father and mother, and anyone who curses father or mother must be put to death. But you say, 'If a man says to his father or mother: Anything I have that I might have used to help you is Corban (that is, dedicated to God), 'then he is forbidden from that moment to do anything for his father or mother.' In this way you make God's word null and void for the sake of your tradition which you have handed down. And you do many other things like this."

Prayer.

  Jesus, knowing that you are the *word* and that you existed before the heavens and earth were even cre-

Are You Sure This Is Mine?

ated—You know that I can't even come close to comprehending that, and that failing to comprehend, I give you my human limitations, limitations that cannot begin to do you justice or give you the glory you deserve. Your spirit, filling the lives of all Christians. Wow. Help me to accept and comprehend that. Help me to know you, not as I have sought to know you which is limiting but as you would have me know you. You alone know how strong-willed I am. Help me to use that to your glory, not mine. That is not going to be easy, Lord, for even now I want to follow my will. Strange, that same thing that gives me strength gives me weakness.

* * * *

Genesis 2:15-17

Yahweh God took the man and settled him in the garden of Eden to cultivate and take care of it. Then Yahweh God gave the man this admonition, "You may eat indeed of all the trees in the garden. Nevertheless of the tree of the knowledge of good and evil you are not to eat, for on the day you eat of it you shall most surely die."

Mark 7:14-23

He called the people to him again and said, "Listen to me, all of you, and understand. Nothing that goes into a man from outside can make him unclean; it is the things that come out of a man that make him un-

Judy Gill Milford

clean. If anyone has ears to hear, let him listen to this."

When he had gone back into the house, away from the crowd, his disciples questioned him about the parable. He said to them, "Do you not understand either? Can you not see that whatever goes into a man from outside cannot make him unclean, because it does not go into his heart but through his stomach and passes out into the sewer?" (Thus he pronounced all foods clean.) And he went on, "It is what comes out of a man that makes him unclean. For it is from within, from men's hearts, that evil intentions emerge: fornication, theft, murder, adultery, avarice, malice, deceit, indecency, envy, slander, pride, folly. All these evil things come from within and make a man unclean."

Prayer.

Lord, I know that it is from within that evil intentions emerge. A lot of these you name are not a problem for me. But we, you and I, know which ones are. You know better than I because you see me struggling along sometimes before I know what I am doing. Help me with the big one, pride.

* * * *

Genesis 2:18, 21-25

Yahweh God said, "It is not good that the man should be alone. I will make him a helpmate . . ."

Are You Sure This Is Mine?

Yahweh God built the rib he had taken from the man into a woman, and brought her to the man. The man exclaimed:

> "This at last is bone from my bones,
> and flesh from my flesh!
> This is to be called woman,
> for this was taken from man."

This is why a man leaves his father and mother and joins himself to his wife, and they become one body.

Prayer.

God, thank you for reminding me that I am to be a helpmate to my husband, that my husband and I are *one body*. I have confidence in myself as a being created by and chosen by you so seeing myself as Rob's helpmate does not threaten me. It does, however, make me realize that sometimes I think of myself first and do not give him the support he requires and deserves. Help me, in the coming weeks when Rob will be so busy to remember that being a helpmate to him is one of the roles that you, God, have given me.

* * * *

Genesis 3:1-9

The serpent was the most subtle of all the wild beasts that Yahweh God had made. It asked the woman, "Did God really say you were not to eat from

Judy Gill Milford

any of the trees in the garden?" The woman answered the serpent, "We may eat the fruit of the trees of the garden. But of the fruit of the tree in the middle of the garden God said, 'You must not eat it, not touch it, under pain of death.'" Then the serpent said to the woman, "No! You will not die! God knows in fact that on the day you eat it your eyes will be opened and you will be like gods, knowing good and evil." The woman saw that the tree was good to eat and pleasing to the eye, and that it was desirable for the knowledge that it could give. So she took some of its fruit and ate it. She gave some also to her husband who was with her, and he ate. Then the eyes of both of them were opened and they realized that they were naked. So they sewed fig leaves together to make themselves loincloths.

Prayer.

God, I read about Eve and I see myself in her. You above all see me as I am. You know that my quest for knowledge like that of Eve does not always lead me closer to you. And yes, if I had to stand before you now, I, too, would want to hide because my flaws and imperfections are much too visible for me to stand before you, Holy Lord, without my being ashamed and wanting to cover my nakedness. Help me to control my quest for knowledge. Help me to be discerning so that my search will lead me, not away, but towards you.

* * * *

Are You Sure This Is Mine?

Genesis 3:9-12

But Yahweh God called to the man. "Where are you?" he asked. "I heard the sound of you in the garden," he replied. "I was afraid because I was naked, so I hid." "Who told you that you were naked?" The man replied, "It was the woman you put with me; she gave me the fruit, and I ate it."

Prayer.

God, you know that like Adam and Eve I sometimes hide, not wanting to do what you ask of me. Help me to know what you want for me and help me to be willing even when it is not what I myself would choose. Help me also to know and to remember that if we trust in you, you will provide for our needs.

* * * *

Sirach (Ecclesiasticus) 15:15-20

> If you wish, you can keep the commandments,
>   to behave faithfully is within your power.
> He has set fire and water before you;
>   put out your hand to whichever you prefer.
> Man has life and death before him;
>   whichever a man likes better will be given him.
> For vast is the wisdom of the Lord;
>   he is almighty and all-seeing.
> His eyes are on those who fear him,
>   he notes every action of man.

Judy Gill Milford

Prayer.

Father, thank you for giving us freedom to choose. You have told us we have the power to be faithful. We are able to choose life or death. Your wisdom is great, oh Lord. You are almighty and all-seeing. You notice my every action. Help me to be strong enough to make choices you would have me make.

* * * *

Genesis 4:2-8

She gave birth to a second child Abel, the brother of Cain. Now Abel became a shepherd and kept flocks, while Cain tilled the soil. Time passed and Cain brought some of the produce of the soil as an offering for Yahweh, while Abel for his part brought the first-born of his flock and some of their fat as well. Yahweh looked with favor on Abel and his offering. But he did not look with favor on Cain and his offering, and Cain was very angry and downcast. Yahweh asked Cain, "Why are you angry and downcast? If you are well disposed, ought you not to lift up your head; But if you are ill disposed, is not sin at the door like a crouching beast hungering for you, which you must master?" Cain said to his brother Abel, "Let us go out"; and while they were in the open country, Cain set on his brother Abel and killed him.

Prayer.

Help me to understand why Cain's offering was not acceptable to God while Abel's was. It makes me

Are You Sure This Is Mine?

angry to read that. I don't want to think that my offering might be less acceptable than someone else's. It hurts my pride to realize that I cannot save myself by my own effort. It is only through faith in you my Lord Jesus Christ that I can be saved. It seems I have to learn that over and over.

* * * *

Genesis 6:5-7

Yahweh saw that the wickedness of man was great on earth and that the thoughts in his heart fashioned nothing but wickedness all day long. Yahweh regretted having made man on the earth, and his heart grieved. "I will rid the earth's face of man, my own creation."

Mark 8:14-21

The disciples had forgotten to take any food and they had only one loaf with them in the boat. Then he gave them this warning, "Keep your eyes open; be on your guard against the yeast of the Pharisees and the yeast of Herod." And they said to one another, "It is because we have no bread." And Jesus knew it, and he said to them, "Why are you talking about having no bread? Do you not yet understand? Have you no perception? Are your minds closed? *Have you eyes that do not see, ears that do not hear?* Or do you not remember? When I broke the five loaves among the five thousand, how many baskets full of scraps did you collect?" They answered, "Twelve." And when I

Judy Gill Milford

broke the seven loaves for the four thousand, how many baskets full of scraps did you collect?" And they answered, "Seven." Then he said to them, "Are you still without perception?"

Prayer.

Jesus, I can see wickedness spreading today as in the time of Noah. Corruption fills the air. I have confidence that one person can make a difference. Help me to have the courage to try, even when it seems my voice won't be heard—even when I wonder what difference it could make. Just as you have told us to watch for the yeast of the evil, you have also reminded us that a small amount will multiply to feed thousands. Thank you for reminding me of the importance of even the smallest deed in influencing others.

* * * *

Mark 8:22-26

They came to Bethsaida, and some people brought to him a blind man whom they begged him to touch. He took the blind man by the hand and led him outside the village. Then putting spittle on his eyes and laying his hands on him, he asked, "Can you see anything?" The man, who was beginning to see, replied, "I can see people: they look like trees to me, but they are walking about." Then he laid his hands on the man's eyes again and he saw clearly; he was

Are You Sure This Is Mine?

cured, and he could see everything plainly and distinctly. And Jesus sent him home, saying, "Do not even go into the village."

Prayer.

Jesus, you know that I seek to really know you above all things and yet that feeling of knowing you always eludes me. Cure me, I ask you, as you did the blind man, of my blindness. Open my eyes that I may see all there is to know of you and that I may live as you would have me live. In your name I ask this.

* * * *

Mark 8:27-33

Jesus and his disciples left for the villages around Caesarea Philippi. On the way he put this question to his disciples, "Who do people say I am?" And they told him. "John the Baptist," they said, "others Elijah; others again, one of the prophets." "But you," he asked, "who do you say I am?" Peter spoke up and said to him, "You are the Christ." And he gave them strict orders not to tell anyone about him.

And he began to teach them that the Son of Man was destined to suffer grievously, to be rejected by the elders and the chief priests and the scribes, and to be put to death, and after three days to rise again; and he said all this quite openly. Then, taking him aside, Peter started to remonstrate with him. But, turning and seeing his disciples, he rebuked Peter and said to him, "Get behind me Satan! Because the way you think is not God's way but man's."

Prayer.

Jesus, I know that so often I am like Peter. The way I think is not your way, but the world's. I want to be Godly, but I call on my own strength instead of yours. Without your life in me I am nothing—helpless. I have no strength that is not your own. I have nothing that you have not given me. Thank you for being with me. Help me to grow in love for you.

* * * *

Mark 8:34-38.

He called the people and his disciples to him and said, "If anyone wants to be a follower of mine, let him renounce himself and take up his cross and follow me. For anyone who wants to save his life will lose it; but anyone who loses his life for my sake, and for the sake of the gospel, will save it. What gain, then, is it for a man to win the whole world and ruin his life? And indeed what can a man offer in exchange for his life?"

Prayer.

Lord, I know, for you have told us plainly, that I must give up my worldly life in order that I may live with you. It is so hard to know just how far I have to go in turning my back on things of this world. Fa-

Are You Sure This Is Mine?

ther, I turn to you for guidance. I know that you will show me, if I will be open to it. Thank you for offering me life and help me to receive it continuously so that I may grow in you.

* * * *

Hebrews 11:1-7

Only faith can guarantee the blessings that we hope for, or prove the existence of the realities that at present remain unseen. It was for faith that our ancestors were commended.

It is by faith that we understand that the world was created by one word from God, so that no apparent cause can account for the things we can see.

It was because of his faith that Abel offered God a better sacrifice than Cain, and for that he was declared to be righteous when God made acknowledgment of his offerings. Though he is dead, he still speaks by faith.

It was because of his faith that Enoch was taken up and did not have to experience death: he was not to be found because God had taken him. This was because before his assumption it is attested that he had pleased God. Now it is impossible to please God without faith, since anyone who comes to him must believe that he exists and rewards those who try to find him.

It was through his faith that Noah, when he had been warned by God of something that had never

Judy Gill Milford

been seen before, felt a holy fear and built an ark to save his family. By his faith the world was convicted, and he was able to claim the righteousness which is the reward of faith.

Prayer.

Father, it is certainly plain looking at Hebrews that the key is *faith,* not feeling. Thank you for suffering for me. I take your suffering for granted. Sometimes, knowing that you are God *and* man, I feel that your suffering was not great when I know that I cannot even conceive of the suffering you experienced. Help me to remember.

* * * *

I have added *Collected Poems* by Karol Wojtyla to my beside book collection. I wish I had written his words:

> The Lord taking root in the heart is a flower
> that longs for the warmth of the sun,
> so flood in light from the day's inconceivable
>   depths
> and lean upon my shore.[2]

* * * *

The relationship that has developed between J.J. and Will amazes me.

Are You Sure This Is Mine?

J.J. was already nine
when the little intruder
came to live with us.
I wasn't sure that it would work.
J.J. liked to sleep undisturbed each morning.
The little intruder cried a lot
and grabbed fistfuls of fur for fun.
But he also trusted completely
and handed generous peace offerings
from his high chair.
A friendship grew.
J.J. is fourteen now.
She doesn't bark at thunder as often as she once did.
This spring when we got out her favorite soccer ball,
she showed no sign of remembering
her love of the chase.
Sometimes, it takes her two, even three tries
to jump on the bed.
But if anyone makes a move against the little intruder,
J.J. is on him with a growl and a snap.
And every morning instead of sleeping
J.J. and the intruder roll around the floor
in a tumble of black and white,
wagging tail and laughter.
Maybe you cannot teach an old dog new tricks,
But you can give an old dog
a new love.

* * * *

Judy Gill Milford

Well, Judy, you've done it again. Here you were keeping the prayer journal, reading the scripture and praying daily. You really thought you were going to stick with it, didn't you? As usual you got busy with other activities and the prayer journal is abandoned. Why do you do this? Why can't you have steady consistent growth and commitment?

* * * *

Attending the catechetical study in March, we were asked to list the gifts that we have received from God, meaning the talents we have received. The gift of loving people, all people, is high on my list. I really felt that I could love anyone.

God, why did you send that young man into my life? You know—the unlovable one, the one whose every word grates against my being, the one I must struggle to be nice to. Before he appeared I felt loving —almost holy. I thought that being able to love all people was one of my gifts. Now, I feel ashamed, I who live in a comfortable home surrounded by friends and loved ones. I congratulate myself for my accomplishments and hesitate to commit myself to tasks beyond my pleasure. Once again, through this boy, you have shown me that some things are beyond my strength. I must call on you to help me love him, to see the beauty and worth in him.

* * * *

Are You Sure This Is Mine?

One secret, I think, to loving people, all people, is to see them not as they are at any given moment, but as the potential of what they can be or what they could have been. People are never just what I see before me today or what I know of them. They are so much more, the sum of their past, present and future. If I take time to make a connection with people in a positive way, I contribute to the people they are to become.

* * * *

The beauty of this day was unsurpassed by any in my memory. With sun shining on new dogwood blossoms, tulips, japonica, I drove around town with the wind whipping in the open sun roof and the sun adding its warmth to everything it touched. I would like to make new words to describe it all. On paper it sounds so ordinary, so everyday and it was anything but that. I was filled with joy.

But, on the other hand, is it somehow wrong for me to feel such elation, such exuberance, when everywhere people are living in pain? How can I revel in the perfection of this day in spring knowing what I know?

* * * *

Judy Gill Milford

The C.P.A.

There's a stranger living in the house
   from January into April.
He eats, sleeps, showers here
   hardly ever talks.
All day he is away.
He rarely calls.
In the evenings after mealtime
his shoulders round the table
over expanding piles of paper
and stacks of forms
until late in the night
with silence interrupted
only by the rhythmic sound of his machine.
Sometimes, he crawls inside himself
and takes to bed with pain and fever
in silent effort
to regain that part of himself
that is being used up much too quickly.
Occasionally, he spends an entire evening with
   me.
We eat. We try to talk, even laugh a little
in conscious effort to regain that part of us
that is being used up much too quickly.
In spite of the effort,
He knows
and I know
That the stranger never leaves
until April 15.

* * * *

Are You Sure This Is Mine?

Sometimes, I have thought of myself and the freedom I get from writing as a bird in flight or perhaps a plane. But I realize that I must be—have to be a kite. I must remain attached to earth—to my family by the string. I must be able to reel myself in, to return to earth, maintain the balance. I cannot let myself break the string and soar without thought of a safe landing.

* * * *

Judy Gill Milford

XII

The fact is, I know of nothing good living in me—living, that is, in my unspiritual self—for though the will to do what is good is in me, the performance is not, with the result that instead of doing the good things I want to do, I carry out the sinful things I do not want. (Romans 7:18,19)

> I suffer pain
> For that which I want to know—I know not.
> That which I want to do—I do not.
> The way I want to live—I live not.
> The way I want to love—I love not.
> The face which I seek remains enshadowed
> And I am nothing
> Seeking something
> Seeking the most powerful, most glorious
> all-knowing, all-seeing God.

* * * *

Are You Sure This Is Mine?

This God of mine insists on humility and dares me to forget that I must rest in him. So many lessons painfully learned and still I venture out like a toddler running into the traffic of a busy street.

* * * *

Rob never told me I was pretty. He never said, "I like your smile," "I like your hair." I am glad for that. If he had said I was beautiful, cute, talented or smart, I might be afraid somewhere deep inside that his love for me was dependent on his perception of the way I look or dress. His failure to compliment and place boundaries is part of the mystery that is our love. He loves me as I am, so I, not knowing why, must be the very best that I can be in every way every minute of every day while at the same time remaining free to change, to grow.

To My Husband—Married to a Poet

The freedom
that you give me
binds me to you in a way
that no chain ever could.
So don't feel threatened
by the other love
that shares our bed,
wakes me from restless sleep,
and calls me into the fragrant bird-song sunrise

Judy Gill Milford

or draws me willfully into the company of
  strangers.
Simply know that I recognize
the confidence you have in me
and in us
as strength.

* * * *

Our pediatrician has died. I didn't want to let him go. I had confidence in him. Even though I knew he had closed his practice, I had not faced the inevitability of his death. If I ever have an incurable illness, I don't want people to give up on me—to think of me as dead before I am gone. I have seen the way they sometimes shake their heads and cluck just like checking someone prematurely off the list of life.

* * * *

I hope I don't live longer than the last gravel road in America. The few I see call out to me like nothing else. An interstate highway or an expressway passes chemical plants, shopping centers and airports, but a gravel road—a gravel road is like a treasure map leading to the unknown.

* * * *

Perhaps I made a mistake.
I said what had to be said

Are You Sure This Is Mine?

and having said it
felt much better.
What a relief to have a burden
reduced to several words
on paper.
So far, so good.
The possible error came in my decision
to share these words with others.
"We regret that we are unable
to find a place for it right now."
With receipt of these words
I re-examine everything
that I have written
find it all wanting,
Remind myself that, after all
I write only for myself,
And resolve never to submit again.
At least not for a while.

* * * *

Yesterday at eleven-thirty we paraded down the walkway to the sand armed with chairs, towels, books for Beth and I, floats for the boys. We had Number 4 suntan lotion for Beth, Chris, Robby, Will and I—Number 15, a hat, shirt and umbrella for Rob (Is it any wonder he prefers the shade?). The scorching sun illuminated my flaws but we were encouraged by hundreds of imperfect bodies planted towel to towel as far as we could see. In spite of repeated warnings about the dangers of unprotected rays, pale

Judy Gill Milford

and tan-shaded bodies swarmed the beaches in search of that miraculous healing warmth. Lying there crowded into my designated spot, nothing seemed new or exciting. The world was overused.

But this morning I approach the waves alone with the sun. I can sympathize with the angry bird who yells "intruder" as he dives the foam in search of food. I am an explorer and the world is new. Playful waves nip my knees like an energetic puppy. I dream of visiting faraway uninhabited islands, of being stranded away from oppressive crowds until I stumble over a Big Mac carton and an empty Miller can. . . .

* * * *

The other day I ran into a high school classmate who I had not seen in years. I stood there chatting, reminiscing—inwardly proud of the growth and development I had achieved through the years, hoping my old friend was able to see that I had changed for the better.

Afterward, it occurred to me that never in thinking of her in the past twenty years had I ever let her exceed the confines of the boundaries of the person that she was the last time I saw her on graduation night, 1966.

* * * *

Are You Sure This Is Mine?

With two of the children in college, the house is quieter and a little cleaner. It sounds silly to admit but sometimes when no one is around, I go into their rooms on the pretext of dusting. With a ceramic birthday angel or an autographed baseball in my hands it is much easier to relive the days that passed too swiftly. I would like to be able to go to the freezer and take out a zip-lock bag of frozen moments, but I know that is no answer to the strange feelings I have when I realize how many years have passed.

* * * *

Beth is so excited. She applied for a credit card, and got it. She fingered the new piece of plastic like a newly found treasure. The importance of a credit card today is frightening to me. In fact, it is a complete mystery. Companies send applications for cards that have not been requested. Credit cards are issued to young people in college. Our young adults are actually being encouraged on every side to spend more than they have or can realistically hope to pay for. What can we do about this?

* * * *

I feel that I am living on the edge of insanity—not mine, the world's. I remember when full-time mothers took pride in their ability to nurture and

Judy Gill Milford

provide a stable home environment. I wonder if that pride will ever live again? All around me women boast and strive to prove their manliness. There is a power struggle going on between male and female and I fear that the competition threatens to contribute to the breakdown of the family as we know it. It is no wonder that there seem to be more problems with sexual identity than ever before. Roles are being tossed about and scrambled for like a prize. I see little common respect and consideration, but a lot of "me first—I want." What is happening? Can good come from this?

* * * *

A friend of ours lost her husband to a heart attack. As I begin to think about her trying to readjust her life and that of her children, I realized that we make subconscious adjustments in life to prepare for the inevitable—few couples die at exactly the same time.

Like teenagers who constantly criticize and berate their parents in an unconscious effort to prove to themselves that they can indeed live without them as adults when the time comes; so I draw back slightly from this love of twenty years, form little pieces of life without him, little areas of apartness that do not include him to convince myself that if someday I had to, I could continue to exist alone.

* * * *

Are You Sure This Is Mine?

In our parish we have an Irish nun who helps to define the word dedication. With a small pouf of red hair coming out of the front of her nun's cap she walks around town briskly taking care of her business in sturdy walking shoes. Although some might have to dodge her sharp tongue, there is a twinkle in her blue eyes and a bit of softness, too, especially around babies.

One morning going into Bible study I heard her mention a terminally ill parishioner who she had just visited. As she spoke of his preparation to "go and meet Jesus," I knew that if I had foreknowledge of my inevitable death, she was the person I would most want beside me cheering me onward to the finish line.

* * * *

Preparing to take Beth for her second year at University of Louisville, I know from last year's experience the emptiness of passing her deserted room, the echo that laughs when I knock at her door before remembering that she is not there. I tell her angrily how glad I am that her bathroom will finally stay clean, what a relief it will be not to have her constant supply of dirty laundry, and how great it will be not to have to wait up until after midnight for her safe return. She tells me indignantly how wonderful it will be to be back at school with her friends, how nice it will be not to have to check in with someone

Judy Gill Milford

when she comes in at night. We go about the necessary, sometimes painful, preparations for our separate lives.

* * * *

One of our sons had a problem over the Labor Day weekend—not a devastating problem, but big enough to make me think. Sometimes reality is sweet to savor, such a treat to hold in the mouth, roll over the taste buds again and again. Other times it is an oversized pill, too large to swallow, that sticks in the throat, will not go away.

* * * *

What element in the September change of wind not yet cool compels the agile squirrel on an expedition of haste? Like a stone skipping a green lake he gracefully scampers to scurry and store. I share certain primeval instincts with him for already the urgency rises within me. I begin the frantic search, although, instead of nuts, my cache is words.

* * * *

Some poems can be read quickly for fun and maybe even a little enlightenment, but the best poems are like a spider spinning a silken thread about me. I am caught in his majestic web—more

Are You Sure This Is Mine?

deeply ensnared with each reading until just in time I wrestle free, a little wiser for my encounter.

* * * *

Aren't some parents doing their children a disservice today by teaching them that the world owes them something instead of teaching responsibility? We had very little when I was young but my mom and dad never told us that other people owed us. Instead they told us that we had the power to change our lives and have more than they had if we worked hard, got a good education and treated others the way we would like to be treated. That combination has proven effective for me.

* * * *

A car and a watch have a lot in common. The car takes me where I need to go. The watch tells me when to get there. As long as they both run, it shouldn't matter if the car is a BMW or VW—or whether the watch is a Rolex or Timex. They both fulfill their purposes.

* * * *

When I get something new, I expect it to last forever. I was annoyed that my yellow robe has frayed sleeves until I realized that I got it to wear in the

Judy Gill Milford

hospital when Robbie (he has recently changed the spelling of his name) was born. He is sixteen. We bought our stereo in the early seventies as a "piece of furniture" that would last. Well, the stereo cabinet is fine, but the system is obsolete. A few years ago the turntable slowed down, needed repair. I was told that the required parts were no longer made so they fixed it the best they could. Now, something else is wrong. And when we replace something, we have so many choices. I wonder if we would be better off with fewer styles and models to choose from, but better quality. In America we have choices. I like them, but many products are put together in such a way that another choice is soon required. No wonder the dumps and landfills are taking over the country.

* * * *

Are You Sure This Is Mine?

XIII

Then Jesus said to his disciples, "I tell you solemnly, it will be hard for a rich man to enter the kingdom of heaven. Yes, I tell you again, it is easier for a camel to pass through the eye of a needle than for a rich man to enter the kingdom of heaven. . . ." "For men," he told them, "this is impossible; for God everything is possible." (Matthew 19:24-26).

GOOD fortune is a cross to bear, for when a person is continually blessed with riches it becomes increasingly difficult to achieve or gain any degree of holiness. Why is it that the better our life is the worse we are? Successful business, healthy children, nice clothes and cars encourage us to become centered on ourselves and turn away from God. When things are going well, it is easy to give ourselves credit and assume that we can handle everything alone.

* * * *

Judy Gill Milford

Most of the time I consider myself a reasonable person. In relation to possessions, however, I have some feelings that are hard to justify. For example, my mom and dad still live in the house that I grew up in (the one that I moved into at three-and-a-half), but I know that if they had to sell it and someone else lived there I would always consider that *my* home. I would want to walk the land, breathe the air and listen to familiar house sounds. I would feel entitled to it.

I feel the same way about my poetry. Once a poem is published it belongs to everyone. Any person anywhere could, if they desired, carry it in their wallet or in their heart. In a way it no longer belongs to me and yet I feel fiercely possessive about the things I have written. I think I understand why Emily kept her poems hidden in a box.

* * * *

I remember when
Santa Claus was real.
I knew exactly how
his house looked
at North Pole, USA,
and would have recognized
any one of his elves.
Once in those days
I saw the Easter Bunny himself
sneaking up our back stairs
with his basket of colored eggs.

Are You Sure This Is Mine?

The Tooth Fairy visited with regularity.
Then one day a classmate told me
that all of these were myths—
that only babies believed.
For years after that
I tossed God back and forth
between fact and fiction
not knowing where he belonged.

* * * *

Why would God make me a perfectionist and give me this to work with?

* * * *

Ordinarily when I meet a person, it is like talking to someone in transition. Not only do I glimpse what he is and what he was but what he can become. Sometimes, I meet a person who is so set on rejecting new thoughts, so locked into his way of thinking that he seems not to hear another voice at all.

* * * *

I forget that some people are inflexible, unyielding, unwilling to proceed. What makes them content to stay in one place, to accept where they are as the only place to be? In some ways I, who am compelled to examine possibilities before accepting truth, envy

Judy Gill Milford

them, but in others I am stifled by their reluctance to grow, by the doors that remain firmly closed in their minds.

What could be worse than a prison of your own making? Were they born with the only set of answers so that there was no need to look further? Were they willing to accept the first answer that came along to every question? or at some time, did they open a door just enough to glimpse something so frightening to them that they knew they could not proceed?

* * * *

What a silly argument with my son about a friend of his who may be using drugs. It was never supposed to be an argument. I just wanted conversation. Concern, on my part for his friend, was misread as judgment. I don't know why he didn't think that I could talk and think objectively about the problem. Why did he assume that I wanted him to reject his friend, not stand by him?

I have to admit that it is a little scary. Our first instinct is to protect our own and we hear so much about peer pressure. Can we be sure who will influence whom? He is strong and has good judgment. I must have enough confidence in him to allow him to stand by and encourage his friend. Wouldn't I want the same for him if he were in trouble?

* * * *

Are You Sure This Is Mine?

For years I served well-balanced meals
with brussel sprouts, asparagus
or casseroles that have the
green things hidden well.
"Nutrition is important for a healthy
mind and body," I would say.
He rejected everything except meat,
potatoes, corn and bread
consistently without relenting
once to taste.
Now after one year of living in a college dorm
with "all the guys"
he is home for the summer.
He is eating green beans, lettuce
and casseroles.
What could be the reason for this change?
Does nine months of cafeteria eating
create a love of vegetables?
Do a boy's friends exert more
influence than twenty years
of a mother's loving care?
or is there a heretofore
undiscovered correlation
between beer-drinking and vegetable eating?

* * * *

I remember an old saying that the "road to hell is paved with good intentions." I don't know if that is true but if it is I am halfway there. Most of the things

Judy Gill Milford

I plan never get done. I have a lifetime supply of greeting cards that have not been mailed. Birthday. Father's Day, Sympathy. The one that makes me feel the worst is the Get Well for the person who has already died.

When my mind starts clicking "Judy, you should . . ." I should begin immediately to take action instead of thinking about it. That way I wouldn't get myself into such guilt-provoking predicaments. Those cards remind me of every procrastinating fault I have.

* * * *

A lot is being written today about guilt. We are told to feel good about ourselves and to do what makes us feel good. That is all right up to a point, but aren't we forgetting something? In Matthew 7:12 Jesus tells us, "so always treat others as you would like them to treat you; that is the meaning of the Lord and the Prophets." If we don't give others that consideration, we should feel guilty. Isn't it important to have guilt long enough to make positive changes, but at the same time be able to let it go once it has served its purpose? Jesus gives us a place to unload our guilt. He has offered relief—that of not carrying the burden of guilt throughout our lives.

* * * *

Are You Sure This Is Mine?

I have been asked to represent Paducah Mother-to-Mother at an IMPACT briefing in Washington, D.C. An inadequate income mother will go too. My first thought was, "Oh, I couldn't possibly, everyone is more qualified than I am," but I started thinking and it sounds great. The topics to be discussed are interesting—children in poverty, hunger in America plus farm crisis, South Africa, Central America, and others. We will learn how to influence congressmen in voting on important issues. I hate politics. I cannot believe I am even thinking about doing this, but it seems right.

Also, I have never flown without Rob, but Tanya, the other woman from Paducah, has not flown at all so I'll have to be the "expert." It will be a real adventure. We will stay at the William Penn House, a bed and breakfast place run by the Quakers right down from the Capitol Building. I am as excited as a little girl!

* * * *

The speaker at the opening service was from South Africa and has been imprisoned for anti-apartheid activities. One of the most moving parts of the service was the sharing of the oranges. Taking a section from an orange in a candlelit church, then passing the remainder to the stranger on the left for her to share all the way down the pew is more effective fel-

Judy Gill Milford

lowship than standing in line for cookies at a noisy reception.

* * * *

Almost every moment is scheduled. There are many sessions—some with choices. I try to choose those of interest to MTM and Paducah Co-operative Ministry. I am hearing so much at once. It is overwhelming. I get the feeling that we are supposed to accept everything we hear as truth, but I know that most if not all of these problems have no easy answers. One thing that bothers me is that so many people here seem to be pro-choice.

* * * *

A group from the briefing will march to the South African embassy in the morning. All who wish to go are encouraged. Our plane is leaving too early for us to participate. The speaker said there would be arrests. It is hard to believe I could be arrested for marching and standing at a building. I wonder what Rob and the children would think about that?

* * * *

Memories of my trip are stored
in careless disarray
like my strangely intermingled mental

Are You Sure This Is Mine?

maze of corridors weaving in and out
of every airport in the land.
William Penn House, once unique
begins to look like other over-nights
in other cities, other years.
Paintings that hung in the
Blue Room on the White House tour
now hang in a grey room in my mind.
Assorted meals and mealtimes
have become one tasteless, colorless
smorgasbord.
The man sleeping
in a wilted refrigerator box
at the entrance to the Metro—
not as easily dismissed . . .

* * * *

I remember springs when fresh pink and white
petals held color for days.
Now, faded dogwood blossoms
wrinkled, wilting, yellowing
sagging, seconds short
surround me.
Is this the year I buy one of those
dowdy skirted swimsuits?
I wish they made a style that
comes a little closer to the knees . . .

* * * *

Judy Gill Milford

Impossible! I would have said three years ago, and yet I did it. I talked to a group of United Methodist Women about our trip to Washington. For a person who faked it through a semester of speech in college and has never spoken in public, it was quite an accomplishment. Having something I believe in to talk about was the key that made it possible.

* * * *

Are You Sure This Is Mine?

XIV

When a man has a great deal given him, a great deal will be demanded of him. (Luke 12:48).

AS A mother in the home every day has been an adventure. I face every day with expectation and the thought that for this day I will accomplish and learn as much as I can. I know that I have been lucky, that not all women have choices. For me this has been a beautiful part of my life.

* * * *

Today, at the mailbox, I got news that a poem was accepted. My mind immediately started checking for someone to report it to. I was so excited—like a child in front of a stack of birthday presents. Rob is out of his office, the children are at school, my best poet friend is wintering in Texas, and none of my other friends would be interested. What is it about good

Judy Gill Milford

news that makes a person want to tell, and having no one to report to, the flavor is diminished?

* * * *

I don't understand why my personal appearance is important to me. I am not the body that I walk around in so why do I want it to look perfect? It does not matter to me what others look like. I accept them whatever, so why do I even spend the smallest part of a day tending to the way I look? For almost as long as I can remember I have looked in the mirror wanting to look pretty or beautiful, knowing that I was not, but still striving to look as good as I possibly could. It just doesn't make sense, does it?

* * * *

I must be honest and admit that I do enjoy looking at lean muscular bodies with broad shoulders or well-formed legs that provide a good foundation for the man. I enjoy looking at good-looking women, too. I look them up and down and think, "There is the body God meant to give me. Someone took it when he wasn't looking."

Why would a woman pursue (or allow herself to be pursued by) a nice-looking man hoping to join him in bed? Isn't every man, no matter what he looks like, just a runny-nosed little boy with skinned knees in the process of growing into a bald-headed toothless

Are You Sure This Is Mine?

octogenarian approaching impotency? It seems to me the only thing worth basing a relationship on is the substance of the inner man.

* * * *

Tonight at the Fifties-Sixties dance for a local charity, I was reminded of something I had forgotten, the problems of dancing. I like to dance if the music is good. It is uplifting, good exercise, and makes me feel good all over, especially if the music is sixties. Most people seem to prefer music from their teens or early twenties. The music is an inexpensive ticket back in time. "Shout" always takes me to a college fraternity dance. "The Wanderer" takes me to the Ballard Memorial gym. Elvis's "Are You Lonesome Tonight?" takes me to one of Jean Geveden's parties, and "Heartbreak Hotel" flies me all the way to sixth grade (not the best time of my life).

Occasionally, someone other than my husband will ask me to dance. For some that is no problem, but it is for me. What do you do with your eyes? Some people play games with their eyes while they're dancing. I'm not a game player so that is no good. If I close my eyes, my partner's wife may think I'm enjoying it—too much. If I stare at his shirt, he will think he has a stain on shirt or tie. If I look over his shoulder, he may think I am sending messages about his dancing to someone behind me. Sometimes, depending on the music, I could do one of those dance

Judy Gill Milford

steps where I turn around and dance with my back to my partner. How do I know if he is still back there? I may be dancing alone. It is a good thing to try to carry on conversation with my partner but usually the music is too loud. I don't like to yell. It is possible, if I am feeling very creative, to incorporate all of the above into one dance, but it is rather exhausting. That brings us back to the safest, most relaxing, most enjoyable—husband-dancing. Is there any reason to put myself through all that other torture?

* * * *

Humans are funny. Have you ever noticed how each of us focuses on something, preferably something we are good at, and we decide that it is the most important part of living? That way we can feel superior to others. It is important for us to feel superior about something. I look around and see many examples (some closer than I like to admit).

1. Education superiors feel smug about the amount of education they have or the degree they have attained.
2. Money superiors are good at making money (or were born with it) so anyone who isn't wealthy isn't up to their standards.
3. Athletic superiors have natural coordination so if you cannot keep up on the field you are not worth much in their eyes.

Are You Sure This Is Mine?

4. Fashion superiors like for people to dress only in latest fashions.
5. Religion superiors firmly believe that theirs is the one true religion and all others do not have the main connection.
6. Race superiors consider their race above all others.
7. Intellectual superiors are conscious of their I.Q. and that of others.

The list goes on and on. Occasionally, we find someone who is not sure if he excels at anything so just to be safe, he hates or ridicules a lot.

* * * *

Gail came into town to spend time with her mother who is in the hospital. I went with her for a visit and am haunted by the conversation I had with Mrs. Parsons.

> "This is not the way it was supposed to be," she said.
> I nodded, thinking that I knew the way she felt.
> She fumbled with the tube that dangled
> by her collarbone, and shook her head.
> We talked a bit about the way
> things used to be.
> "That graduation brunch you gave us back in '62 was great," I said.

Judy Gill Milford

Her blue eyes sparkled momentary youth
as she agreed that it was rather nice,
then laughed apologetically for being proud.
Then, to her daughter,
"Are you sure you bought
those Christmas gifts for me to give?" she asked,
rubbing bruises on her wrists and hands.
Traditions are important, we agreed,
but hard to keep
as time goes on.
"I never thought
that it would be like this," she said.

* * * *

Crowded into the hotel elevator with twelve to fourteen fraternity men and dates with arms full of drinks and coolers, Rob and I cast knowing glances at each other. We realize the folly of their ways. Beth is visibly annoyed with us for scorning them. Can't she allow us the luxury of being a little smug? We stand here knowing that part of our life is over, the exuberance and excitement of youth. There must be some compensations for our position of being on the far side of forty.

* * * *

I know it is silly and unreasonable, but I cannot tolerate snakes. I let tadpoles become frogs on my kitchen cabinet, I entrapped a praying mantis and

Are You Sure This Is Mine?

caught and fed him live insects for a week before setting him free so that the children could learn about the insect world, but the idea of a snake keeps me out of the most interesting and exciting places. I would do almost anything for my children but that does not include entertaining snakes.

* * * *

The parents' most important function is to help their children find tools with which to cultivate their lives. If I could give these tools as gifts, I would give patience. Patience is important to complete daily tasks, to avoid accidents, and proves most valuable on long-term projects. Patience enables us to work hard for things which will pay off later. We avoid debts by waiting until we have money to pay for something before purchasing. We avoid problems brought on by premature involvement with the opposite sex if we have patience to wait. Patience is valuable to all ages.

Another important tool that I would give is humor. Humor is essential in enabling us to maintain a healthy balance in our lives. If we can laugh at ourselves and our mistakes, we do not take ourselves too seriously so we can handle all the crazy things that happen to us throughout life.

Faith is the most important tool of all. No matter how bad things get or how severe the misfortunes, we will be strong if our faith is secure.

* * * *

Judy Gill Milford

I travel down each path with my children
reluctantly yet sure that I must share their pain.
All the while I know that when grief calls my
    name,
I stand alone.

* * * *

As far as I can tell, competition serves little purpose for me. The only joys worth counting are those which do not detract from someone else. When the source of happiness is winning, it only means that others have lost. How can one be truly happy knowing that others suffered loss and disappointment because of you?

* * * *

I love playing tennis. I'm not sure why except that I know that it is not the competition that attracts me. I rarely win and I don't even care. I really like to hit that little ball. The only time I mind losing is when I am playing in a league. I can't stand that "Oh no, is she in our group again" look in their eyes. It took me a long time to realize that one reason I lost so much was that everyone else hit the ball *away* from their opponent to win a point while I hit the ball *to* mine to keep the ball in play.

I took a couple of lessons once but decided it was wasted money. My left arm has no idea what my

Are You Sure This Is Mine?

right foot is doing and neither knows which way my racket head is facing. If God had wanted me to be a great tennis player, he would have told me these things instead of gifting me with the ability to remember every stupid mistake I have made since I was three.

* * * *

Reading *The Man Who Cried I Am* by John Williams forced me to look at Americanism in a different way—that of a black American. Most Americans, even if they know little about their actual ancestors, assume that somewhere along the line of forerunners, some of them came to America seeking freedom. Black Americans on the other hand assume that their ancestors lost their freedom in coming here. That knowledge puts an entirely different slant on things. Wouldn't that naturally diminish the pride that they feel? If we are to live and work together equally for the success and growth of all, we need to find a way to restore the pride of *all* Americans in their country.

* * * *

Many of the writers here at the retreat write novels or plays in addition to poetry. Sitting around listening to them involved in storytelling I know that the fantasies that are a part of them are unnatural to me. Most of my thinking involves my search for answers.

Judy Gill Milford

The only book that I could write would be that of the journey of my search for God and truth.

* * * *

The critiquing sessions are valuable for me. It is hard to be objective with my own work. When I first write something it is such a relief to get the feelings out of me onto paper that I feel good about the poem for a while. I was the same way when I was painting. Pictures in place of the blank canvas made me feel wonderful. Later, I could stand back and realize that the painting needed quite a bit of work. Critiquing sessions help to speed up the revision process.

* * * *

I sometimes feel I was always the same person, the same person I remember being at three—thinking, questioning, alive. I now know that is not true. There is a time in between when I was different—the time when I was controlled by learned fears: fear of being laughed at, fear of looking funny, fear of not being able to think of something to say, fear of not having the right answer, and on and on. Yesterday, on stage, I was that person again, the person I did not know still exists, the one who panics, who is not in control, who is not free.

* * * *

Are You Sure This Is Mine?

Eight years ago today Dorothy died. When death came unexpectedly to bring relief for all her pain, I blessed God's plan, but now I wish that she were here to see what beautiful young adults her grandchildren have grown to be. She would be proud of these handsome young men, and this confident young woman. And Will, the one who came late, after her death—he would be a joy to her, too. I would like to think she knows. A special joy of heaven would be to see happiness in our loved ones.

* * * *

Am I a selfish person because the person I love treats me well? He is thoughtful, caring, considerate. He gives me freedom—to be silent or loud, active or still. Is my love conditional? If he treated me shabbily, would my feelings for him change? Sometimes, I think they would for everything upon which our relationship is based would shift. When a woman loves a scoundrel, is the love a fiercer, nobler love than when a woman loves a noble man?

* * * *

Writing is a method of getting in touch with my feelings. Ideas focus, new thoughts emerge as old ones are recorded. Writing is a freedom to feel.

* * * *

Judy Gill Milford

One evening well into the TV season a couple of years ago I watched an episode of *Spenser for Hire* expecting to find it like every other TV detective show. I had a pleasant surprise. When it got to the part where detective meets beautiful young woman in distress, instead of ending up in her bed (or she in his), as we see so often these days, Spenser told the young women that he had a commitment to someone who meant a lot to him. I wanted to stand up and cheer. The applause, however, would have been premature. By the next season, the format was changed. Spenser no longer had this long-term commitment. Someone decided that the story line was not exciting enough with a one-woman-love. And so it goes. . . . Would it make a difference if hundreds, even thousands of us said, "We want to see commitments honored on TV?" If I had written praising the show as it was, and others did, too, would executives then know that some of us are tired of the junk that is being fed to our children and would like to see some old-fashioned values? Does anyone want to see old-fashioned values?

* * * *

Strange, the way things happen sometimes. Lifestyles have changed so much in my lifetime that normal has almost reached abnormal and the other way around. It almost makes me angry to know that I am

Are You Sure This Is Mine?

scorned and deemed not "real" just because over twenty years ago I was fortunate enough to have acquired a considerate husband.

* * * *

Judy Gill Milford

XV

How long, Yahweh, am I to cry for help while you will not listen;
to cry "Oppression!" in your ear and you will not save?
Why do you set injustice before me,
why do you look on where there is tyranny?
Outrage and violence, this is all I see, all is contention, and discord flourishes.
And so the law loses its hold, and justice never shows itself.
Yes, the wicked man gets the better of the upright,
and so justice is seen to be distorted. (Habakkuk 1: 2-4).

TODAY is Will's first day of school. People ask me what I am going to do all day. I tell them, clean the house, but I think, "What I really want to do is write."

Besides this isn't the first time I have started my baby in first grade. I did all this ten years ago with Robby. In fact right after that I started writing

Are You Sure This Is Mine?

poetry. I thrive on thinking time. That doesn't mean that I haven't enjoyed Will. The time I spend with him is valuable time but I need some other space for me.

* * * *

Suppose there are two mothers—one who loves and cares for her children, supports them in every way she can; the other has little time for her children, leaves them to fend for themselves. Sometimes, the child of the caring mother develops into a thoughtless adult while the other child adores his mother, is compassionate and kind. Does that make the latter a better mother? Can there ever be a yardstick by which to measure? Where does the truth lie?

* * * *

Today in the checkout line at Wal-Mart an older lady directly in front of me had difficulty getting an out-of-town check approved. That was not too extraordinary until the woman gave her birthdate for added identification. This "older lady" was born three years after me. That must mean that I am old! and yet I am the same as always, aren't I? Have I really changed that much?

* * * *

Judy Gill Milford

Will and I were talking about things that God made. He asked, "Did the devil make fire?" I tell him that God made all things and they are good, as he made them. Things become bad when they are misused or out of control.

"Who made the devil?" he then asked. Children can get to the heart of things quickly. That question still gives me trouble. I know that the devil or Satan supposedly was an angel who fell or chose worldliness over obedience to God.

I get confused when I think about Satan or try to imagine the very concept of him. I can think of God as a reality, but not Satan. I prefer to think of him as a symbol for evil, but if I consider Satan symbol for evil, do I at the same time reduce God to "symbol for good"? I know that God has ultimate power over Satan but I certainly see the devil's influence in the world—in my life. I think he knows my weaknesses better than I know them myself. I make the same mistakes over and over.

* * * *

I just finished reading an article in September, 1988, *Liguorian* by Philip St. Romain, "Journey to the Center of Your Soul." I knew immediately that I must read it—my journey is difficult. One third through the article I found myself, or my problem. On a scale of one to five we were to evaluate the importance of the following items:

Are You Sure This Is Mine?

1. Materialistic security—no problem. (Probably because I have security)
2. Power—Who needs it?
3. Pleasure—Well, I might eat a little compulsively.
4. Other people—I'm sort of like Will Rogers.
5. Work/career. No.
6. Narcissistic self-concern; pride, being "right and perfect." There I am right there. That is where I am most centered. My problems come back to pride over and over.
7. Family—Fair amount of centering here—that's not too bad, is it?
8. Faith—Placing God first. I wonder if I get any points for placing him third.

Then Romain asks the question, "What consequences are you paying because of your attachment to this center?"[1] I can answer that one. I wake up every morning to a sense of loss knowing that I am not centered on God.

"Metanoia" (making the love of God and the desire to do God's will your center and uprooting anything that stands in the way of this God-centeredness)[2] is a constant battlefield for me.

Romain says that it is easy to become uncentered and that sometimes he must surrender his day to God many times. I needed that encouragement—knowing that for others it is hard, too.

* * * *

Judy Gill Milford

My journey into discovery of self is much too slow, but that is because my ego is waging such a battle. I can not let go of my Self.

* * * *

In *A Third Testament* by Malcolm Muggeridge, I am reading about William Blake as the first of the Romantic poets. Muggeridge said that Blake "foresaw with remarkable prescience the industrial revolution that lay ahead."[3] If he saw the progress in his day as an abomination, imagine what he would feel if he were alive today. Blake was right when he said that the machine would "smother the imagination whereby man's creativity could relate itself to God."[4]

I love my life, my family and this earth, and what I see being done to it scares me. Sometimes, I feel that I should not have been born in this century. We are using up the earth much too fast. Will there be anything worthwhile for my children and grandchildren. Is there any way short of a national disaster to convince people that we must change our lifestyles? We must stop polluting. We must stop living for self. I am as guilty as most. I live comfortably and enjoy it.

My faith in God's infinite goodness and wisdom is the only thing that gives me any hope for the future. Without faith in God as our supreme being, the future of the world looks dismal, and without possibility for survival. Faith gives an order to things that can be found in no other way.

* * * *

Are You Sure This Is Mine?

If the earth as we know it were to be destroyed, leaving only a few people to repopulate, I would have greater hope for humanity if our art, music and literature were preserved than if our entire body of scientific knowledge were available to them.

However, if conditions were such that beauty of nature as we know it was forever destroyed, perhaps it would be easier to live without our arts as a reminder of what had been lost. I don't think I could live in a world without the arts, for that is where all truth—the essence of humanity itself lies.

* * * *

Tonight, I watched part of a TV program hosted by Hugh Downs about America. I had to leave the room. Viewing the effect of acid rain on maple trees and the maple syrup industry (our grandchildren may only hear about real maple syrup) is not pleasant. Other scenes were much more frightening. Animals, dead or dying because of entrapment in plastic packages which have washed up on the beaches, toxic wastes dumped into all of our waters making them unsafe for swimming but most important for drinking and for marine life, air unfit for humans or any form of life to breathe because of garbage forced into it each day at an astounding rate. The list goes on. Is this what we call progress?

* * * *

Judy Gill Milford

If I as a person non-involved in direct major pollution feel guilty about what we are doing to our land, how difficult it must be for politicians, executives and owners of companies to live with themselves. It must be painful for them to be alone with themselves when the lights go out at night.

* * * *

How does the attitude toward putting out fires in the national parks (put out only those started by man in order to protect balance of nature) relate to our treatment of man in relation to medicine? One of the problems of the world today is overpopulation. We save and prolong lives through science. Has this contributed to our overall imbalance? We have a moral obligation to save lives. We have, also, a moral obligation to save our planet. How is this to be done?

* * * *

When people are born, I think they come packaged with a personal set of questions that they will ask over and over intermittently throughout their lives. I envy the person with an easy set:

1. Why isn't my hair blond and my body perfect?
2. Why can't I use that car parked out on the street?
3. Why can't I take money from the company, nobody would know?

Are You Sure This Is Mine?

4. Why can't I sleep with Sam's wife?
5. Why bother to get married at all?

They think they have it rough. I would trade sets with them in a minute. My set says things like:

1. Why do good people die young?
2. Why do some people suffer so much?
3. How much is enough?
4. God, are you real?
5. Jesus, I want to be Christlike, why are you still like a stranger to me?
6. Why are there no easy answers?

* * * *

I grew up with the thought in mind that with an education, I could have a successful life, raise my status in society, have conveniences my parents never had. By these standards my life has exceeded all expectations and dreams. From a B.A., a new marriage, and one red Volkswagon, we progressed to two, then three cars, a comfortable home and four children. Busy years have brought few regrets—until now.

In some ways I wish I had never attended the IMPACT briefing in Washington. In many ways I was happier worrying about who's driving to Cub Scouts, what day I clean the Charity League house and who's moving up and down in the Country Club tennis league. I didn't want to be reminded that our

Judy Gill Milford

streams are polluted, children are hungry and entire families are without homes. I wish that I had never learned that the ozone hole is growing or that many people work full-time at minimum wage and still cannot live above the poverty level.

I'm amazed that I was able to live happily as long as I did—oblivious to facts. Oh, I cared about others. I always cared. I just didn't think there was anything I could do besides giving to and working for charities.

My attitude has changed. In the past because I did nothing wrong, I felt innocent. Now, because I do nothing, I feel guilty. I feel responsible. Somehow, we must convince the people of our country that if we do not do something we will lose everything.

We must pass mandatory recycling laws. We must shut down companies which are polluting our air and land even if it means living in a more primitive manner. Will people ever willingly do this? or will we continue on as we are until it is too late? Why are there no easy answers?

* * * *

I've discovered something about myself and food. Usually when I eat between meals, it is a result of thinking about a particular food for a period of time. I begin to visualize some available food and don't rest until I have it. The more I think about it and the way it will taste, the surer I am that I will eat it as soon as possible. Right now I have my mind focused

Are You Sure This Is Mine?

on an ice cream drumstick in the freezer. Instead of allowing myself to think about the drumstick, I switch and allow myself only to think about carrot sticks or a can of asparagus. I tell myself that is all that is available to me until I begin to focus on carrot sticks and asparagus. The trick to controlling food intake is to control your mind. Allow yourself to visualize only nutritious, healthy foods. We have the power to control our desires by fixing our minds on something that we know is acceptable instead of tantalizing ourselves with fantasies about the forbidden.

* * * *

Why have I gained weight?

1. Infrequent exercise.
2. Eating after being full at mealtimes.
3. Nibbling when not particularly hungry.
4. To gain a bigger chest.
5. To plump my cheeks.
6. Conscious raising of my sub-conscious plateau to allow for all of the above.

What to do about weight gain.

1. Exercise daily or at least 3 or 4 days weekly.
2. Don't eat unless really hungry.
3. Don't continue eating after full.
4. Eat only what I really want and "love."
5. Don't eat between meals unless nutritious.

* * * *

Judy Gill Milford

Dietary Resolve

I've had my fill of fatty foods.
I'm going on a diet.
If someone offers a dessert
I will not even try it.
These dimpled thighs are past their prime
There's bulge on left and right
And what one sees as I depart
Is not a pretty sight.
I'll not be tempted by the junk
That formerly I craved.
A person that attached to food
Just has to be depraved.
The time to start is right away.
I will not wait 'til Monday
But first, I'd like to savor
Just one more hot fudge sundae.

* * * *

If I sympathize with someone, suffer pain with them because of their loss, and then write about that pain, is it wrong? Is it wrong to share it with others so that others can understand, or is it somehow infringing on their loss, capitalizing on their pain? I would never want to do that.

* * * *

Are You Sure This Is Mine?

Sometimes, it bothers me that none of our children seem to share my passion for the earth and its beauty, but I am coming to realize that it is hard to survive in the modern world. Maybe the youth of today have to be the way they are to make it. I grieve for the death of beauty and the loss of hope.

* * * *

Since most people think bad things happen to the other person it is probably going to happen to me. If I expect to win, I won't. If I'm watching for something, it won't come. These are three assumptions that I take for granted. This may sound pessimistic to some, but it serves me rather well. If I follow this philosophy, I am rarely disappointed, and I am prepared for anything that may come my way. Sometimes, I even get pleasant surprises.

* * * *

We have an angry society. Man-hating women are busy trying to prove that they can be better than men. Men are angry at women for degrading them and competing so they strive to be better parents or nurturers. Why can't men and women alike accept the fact that physically they are different so therefore sometimes they are best suited for different roles? Oh, I know there are injustices and inequalities that

Judy Gill Milford

need to be changed but this whole male-female problem has gotten out of hand with a vicious cycle of competition. It is all right that women want equal wages as men for the same job done. It is great that men try to spend more time with their children, but aren't a lot of the attitudes all wrong?

* * * *

Knowing myself so well I am too aware of my weaknesses to dream a dream of greatness. Perhaps, the people who reach for stars and grasp them are those who are blind to themselves so that they are not confined to their own concept of self.

* * * *

I was thinking again about something that I've known instinctively for some time, but never put in words. In many ways I'm more connected to the person I was at three or four than the one I was at eight, nine or ten. Before I started school, I was me, but something happened along about six when I started to become what I thought I was supposed to be—what it seemed others expected me to be. Since different people expected different things, it took a while for me to find out who I really am. As soon as I began to emerge, there I was—that very same person I started out with in my earliest recollections of

Are You Sure This Is Mine?

thinking. Five to six years of being, followed by twelve to sixteen years of existence striving to become, with everything that followed the real me once more coming out.

* * * *

Will had a book from the school library that showed the four stages of the butterfly. I think I am in the chrysalis stage—my covering is transparent with my real being shining through mostly visible. Soon I will break loose and fly.

* * * *

I am taking a photography class to learn how to use Rob's 35mm camera. Photography can be as important as writing or painting to express emotion or make a statement. I wish I had learned it years ago. I could have taken more pictures of the kids growing up. I need a longer lens to take many of the pictures I would like, but those powerful lenses are expensive. For now I will just learn the basics and practice, practice, practice. It takes me five minutes to focus. Most of my subjects cannot be still that long (nature and children). Expressions and movements of young children are spontaneous and unpretentious—a statement of truth, like a poem.

* * * *

Judy Gill Milford

Oh God. I seek your face. Yet, I keep my own ever before me. I know that man can serve only one god. I try to serve you but other things get in the way. Sometimes, it is family—a lot of times.

Now, more than ever I must guard against writing becoming the god. It becomes more and more important to me. How can a writer or any artist be holy? All work must be dedicated to you and I forget that. Work that begins as an effort to glorify you becomes, without my realizing it, an effort to glorify the art or myself.

* * * *

Knowing that I am not alone in this concern does not help to solve the problem. Thomas Merton questioned whether his writing honored God, or whether it was simply a celebration of self.[5]

* * * *

How much is enough? God wants, expects much of me. He has called me to holiness. As long as there is hunger and pain among men, how can I rest? How can I be happy? If I give only as it is comfortable for me to give, surely, I have not done enough for my brothers. What does God want of me?

And in giving, how do I know how and where? Some gifts of charity do not go where the giver in-

Are You Sure This Is Mine?

tends. They only end up with the greedy. How does one guard against this?

Giving of myself on a personal level is always safe, isn't it? Even then, how much is enough? Sometimes, people can give so much of themselves that there is no energy left to be. The key, I would guess, is to rely totally on God's wisdom and strength. It is when I rely on my strength that I become weak and make unwise choices.

* * * *

I have been offered a temporary job as an aide at Morgan Elementary School. I would be working with three and four second-graders at a time. I don't know whether to accept. I was prepared to substitute but I had no intention of working full-time. The hours will be the same as Will's so that part is perfect, but am I ready to give up my solitude—my thinking time?

* * * *

Once again the Christmas season approaches
Saturday, police arrested 77 anti-abortion
protesters for blocking a clinic in Cincinnati
while singing Christmas carols.
Marchers carried signs that read:
"Warning: Killing babies

Judy Gill Milford

May be hazardous to your soul."
I think about the desperate
young girls blocked from their destination
by the protestors—
and wonder where we would be today
if another unmarried,
very young woman
some 2,000 years ago
had been
pro-choice.

* * * *

    I don't recall a single Christmas as a child when I didn't experience a great disappointed let-down feeling on Christmas afternoon. Because we didn't have much money, Mom and Dad seldom bought brand names so often the doll didn't look like I expected it to or the sweater wasn't as bright as the ones the other girls had. The main problem though was that nothing could possibly measure up to the fantasy that mushrooms in a child's mind in anticipation of a special event.

    Now at forty-four the special magic anticipation is gone, but so is the hollow disappointment. Being an adult means that for our twenty-two years of marriage there have been no hollow Christmas afternoons. Every Christmas I am filled with thankfulness for this family and every year the greatest pleasure is buying gifts for the ones I love. I will never forget the

Are You Sure This Is Mine?

year Rob said we had enough money to buy my mom the dishwasher she had always wanted. Giving is the excitement and magic of Christmas.

* * * *

Thomas Merton points out something of great importance to us, something I had not thought of myself concerning the birth of Jesus:

> ". . . in this narrative of the miraculous virgin birth of the Lord, as recited in the early Church, we have a revelation of the infinite motherly compassion of God for men, a revelation which is not only absolutely without error but which, by reason of the special "feminine" cast of its literary expression, tells us something quite unique that we would otherwise never comprehend. (Modern psychology makes us aware, for example, of the severe limitations of a theology built exclusively on an authoritarian father-image, and the importance of a concept of sonship in which the mysteries of the Mother and of the Holy Spirit are needed to fill out the full meaning of the redemptive love of the Savior on the Cross."[6]

* * * *

Part Six

Don't Tip the Scales

XVI

I have loved you with an everlasting love, so I am constant in my affection for you. (Jeremiah 31:3)

I REMEMBER the closeness that John and I shared a few years ago before Will was born. We don't have a chance to talk as much now so we are not sharing with each other on a regular basis. I know that I still have the same love for him even though our situations have changed. I think this situation compares to my relationship with God. I remember and long for the closeness that I no longer feel. However, love and commitment are still there. If I make opportunities for sharing, the feelings will return. I must not despair because they are not present right now at this moment.

* * * *

I cannot rely on feelings. Feelings are fickle. I must remind myself daily of my commitment to God—my determination to persevere above all else. Maybe in

Judy Gill Milford

doing that I will find the love and devotion that I seek.

* * * *

As I get older I resent the time I waste grocery shopping. I'm beginning to understand why some older people lose their appetites and quit eating.

* * * *

What is it about the human body that brings a sudden surge forward in the aging process at forty? Maybe the acceleration acts as a caution light telling people to slow down and be alert to things which are likely to approach just ahead. Just like the caution light at a busy intersection, these warning signs cause some people to speed through in an attempt to beat the Stop and causes others to break unnecessarily before their time.

* * * *

Why do the thrill-seekers try to enforce their way of life on others? I remember being called a "scaredy-cat" for not riding the roller coaster at Noble Park when I was a young girl. (We are not even going to discuss the Cannonball or Space Mountain.) A few adventuresome kids actually made me feel guilty (the word now would be wimpy) for not riding in one of

Are You Sure This Is Mine?

those creaking carts a few feet off the ground back in 1959. It took me until I was forty to be able to say, "I don't enjoy, so why ride?" The point in going to an amusement park is to be amused—right? So why should I pay to ride something that gives me no pleasure so that someone else can be amused watching me be miserable?

* * * *

In a short time "wimpy" has become one of the most overused words in our language. I hear it used mostly to describe men. From what I observe, many times it is used by people who make a big show of living to describe someone who goes about things in a quiet way. Many of the quieter people like my dad and Rob exhibit an inner strength that I find lacking in men who must make a big noise. Self-control is an important part of strength.

* * * *

Man of the Earth

Man of the earth
  with hands of a worker
  scarred by the hammer
  browned by the sun
Tiller of soil
  with hands ever-moving

Judy Gill Milford

   pulling the weed
   working the hoe
Model for mankind
   speaks with the animals
   handling gently
   with trust and with love
Man who like granite
   stands uncorrupted
   unchanged by the world
   unweathered by time
Man of integrity
   walks through the day
   with strength born of silence
   with faith that is simple
This man of the earth
This father of mine

* * * *

In spite of jokes about Basketweaving 101 and the raised eyebrows of my friends if they knew, I have a secret desire to make baskets. There is something enticing about making a useful, decorative basket from natural, earthbound materials. I think it would be almost like taking part in nature itself. To feel the materials twist and intertwine amongst themselves within my fingers, transforming it all into a vessel for holding eggs, pine cones, flowers or berries, that is excitement.

* * * *

Are You Sure This Is Mine?

Today I heard a classical piece on the radio that reminded me of the movie *Amadeus*, about the life of Mozart. I would like to be able to identify with Mozart—to know that I could write great music. Maybe I would be as nonchalant as he was portrayed in the movie if I were that gifted. Watching the movie, I identified with Salieri. I have lived with the frustration of mediocrity and I can appreciate the madness he experienced from watching Mozart. All my life I have known my limitations and am stifled by them.

If only I could write one great piece of music, I would write with the passion of Chopin. When I was a young girl I saw a movie called *A Song to Remember* with Cornel Wilde as Chopin and Jose Iturbi as his fingers. Chopin's music has been a vital part of my life since then. It does not matter to me that Chopin is not popular today or that some of his more famous pieces accompany cartoons. When I listen to his works I become a part of them. Each one is new.

* * * *

Sometimes, frivolous nonsensical questions come to my mind like:

1. Is there anything that can be done about that sprinkly mustache that a thirteen or fourteen-year-old boy is apt to wear (the one that makes his face look dirty)? Someone should market a sign, pin or shirt reading, "I shaved

Judy Gill Milford

this morning." That way the boy could shave it off—he wouldn't need it for advertisement.
2. If a man has intelligence and a fly has none, why can a fly find his way out of my kitchen when I pick up the fly-swatter when I cannot find my way unassisted from the doctor's examining room to his outer office?
3. If a woman is born with all the eggs that are later to be used at conception of her children, is there a relationship between the potential life expectancy of a person and the age of his mother at the time of his conception?
4. Can an egg ever split before fertilization and be fertilized by two separate sperm thus producing half-identical twins—those who were formed from a single egg but two separate sperm?

* * * *

Returning to the dorm late one night twenty-five years ago the dorm mother asked if I had been at the school dance and I said, "yes." That part was true, but I did not continue to tell her that I left and went to another in a nearby town. I didn't want her to be disappointed in me and I didn't want to get the other girl in trouble, the one I went with. The memory of that lie is still painful. The question is this: would I have learned more if I had told the truth at that moment

Are You Sure This Is Mine?

and borne the consequences of the infraction than from having hidden it and borne the guilt all these years? And if I learned more from having lied, does that ever justify the lie?

* * * *

Thinking about that incident makes me realize trust is fragile. If the dorm mother knew I lied, she would not have trusted me—maybe ever again. And yet that one lie had a profound effect on me. There were no others and twenty-five years later, I still feel diminished by it.

* * * *

Why do I have the foolish notion that I can communicate with animals? I talk to the animals in the neighborhood as if they are human. I cannot dismiss the feeling that if I put out my hand and speak, the squirrel, cardinal or mockingbird will know exactly what I mean. After forty-five years I am still surprised when they fly away.

* * * *

Some say that my mom was a foreigner, a
"damn yankee"—
   that she never belonged here.
No matter; no matter that she

Judy Gill Milford

was raised in New Jersey
that her dad was Pennsylvania Dutch
or that all she knew until she was twenty
was big city life.
What really counts is scrub-board laundry,
  the cistern she helped dig
  the concrete she helped pour
  biscuits she learned to make "just like Mom's"
  vegetables canned hour after hour
    in unconditioned heat
  the home-grown vegetable and polk green
  summer
  and all those wonderful lean years of kerosene
  lamps
  and outhouses that are so much easier
  to look back on than to live with.
What counts is that she was so proud
  to be living in the country
  that she never complained.
What counts is forty-six years of
  love and loyalty
  to the same man and his Kentucky home.

* * * *

    Thinking about my mom now I realize something I never knew and am somewhat appalled at the realization. Maybe we all do this without realizing it. I have always competed with her. Why would there be competition? And yet in a way there is. Subcon-

Are You Sure This Is Mine?

sciously, I strive to be all the good things that she was, while at the same time I hold her faults to scrutiny and vow that I will never make those same mistakes.

* * * *

What do you say to someone who is grieving for a lost family member or other loved one? Nothing is adequate.

Tell them you know how they feel—they know you don't unless you too have experienced their loss.

Tell them they are lucky the person is no longer suffering—they don't feel very lucky.

Tell them they will feel better in time—that is little consolation for the pain they are now carrying.

So often we say the wrong thing and sometimes we say nothing. I am haunted by my failure to come up with the right words to comfort another mother although her loss came over a year ago.

> Her son is dead.
> He shot himself
> And no one understands
> Why one so young
> Would want to end.
> They say that he played D and D—too much.
> I have a son his age who used to play.
> I am compelled
> To try to know how she
> Must feel to live her pain.

Judy Gill Milford

I know I can't come close and I am glad.
In truth I cannot bear to crawl inside her grief.
Dressing for the funeral
I try on words of consolation.
And now she is before me.
I search her face
For an invitation to speak,
Something to say
To help her continue
Without fracturing the fragile shell.
My carefully chosen condolences
Are cast aside like
Inappropriate clothing.
I say "Hello"
And walk away.

* * * *

St. Augustine once said, "If Christ were standing here with us, what should we feel, not about him, but about ourselves?" I know the answer to that. I would feel exposed, naked—like Adam and Eve must have felt in the garden when God called out to them and they sought to cover their nakedness. I would probably say, "Is time already up? I'm not ready yet. I planned to be a little more perfect before I stood before you. Could you possibly wait and come back in a couple more days?"

* * * *

Are You Sure This Is Mine?

"Oh Lord, I am not worthy, but only say the word and I shall be healed." Of all the unworthy, I am the most. If I say the words and want the healing with my whole heart, should I seek it? or should I stay away because I am so unworthy?

* * * *

I had a very strange dream last night. It was a relief to be out of it. I was caught up in the cooking of that meal—the meat, the carrots vichy with the torn recipe, and the broccoli. I fixed and fixed and fixed. The carrots became mush while I tried to get stems off the broccoli. I couldn't get finished and why did Rob put the Christmas tree back up at this time of year? I pulled something down from the top of the refrigerator and found two size three outfits for Beth that I cut out and never made. The dream. The dream. Why should I fix a meal that wouldn't finish for someone who has been dead for almost nine years? Grandma Swoboda was even there and she has been dead longer.

* * * *

I am learning that I do not have to feel guilty for my sinful nature. I will continue to sin because I am human but I am not a slave to that sin, therefore, I do not need to continue to degrade myself because of it. To do that is self-destructive.

* * * *

Judy Gill Milford

Everything we do affects someone. Thirty-six years ago a new girl came to our third grade class. Vivian Overton stayed only long enough to be in the class picture and imprint herself in my memory forever. I know nothing about what happened to her but I always think of her fondly and with well-wishes because she shared something with me that was unheard of in our part of Kentucky in the early fifties—a pomegranate. I still remember sitting on the ground with her at recess as she handed me those amazing juicy little red seeds.

* * * *

I wonder which affected my life more, Vivian with her act of friendship, or those boys who used to snicker and make fun? Did my accomplishments come because I had to prove something to the boys or would they have come easier and sooner had I not been laughed at?

* * * *

My desire to help these children makes me feel that my job as an aide is worthwhile. If I am able to connect with them in a way that makes them feel acceptable, confident, able to achieve, then surely it can make a difference for at least some of them. I remember the teachers I had who believed in me. I know that they contributed to the person that I am today.

Are You Sure This Is Mine?

How can a teacher, or any person, intentionally treat a child in a manner that would degrade him and diminish his capacity to achieve?

* * * *

Doing lunchroom duty for the third grade class, I see a lifetime of experience and pain looking out at me from eight and nine-year-old eyes. I grieve for childhoods that were never allowed to be—futures that will never develop. It is not fair that some children are robbed of their childhood before they have a chance to see what it is about. Can't we do something to break the destructive cycle of some people's lives?

* * * *

I think God is the ultimate Game Master. To each person he passes out a Game of Life. Some games come equipped with the correct set of answers, some have an incorrect or partially correct set. Mine has none.

* * * *

Why am I a person with all questions and no answers? I search for answers and being unable to find them, settle into inactivity.

* * * *

Judy Gill Milford

At the writer's retreat this weekend, I observed several kinds of people:

1. Those who came to *learn* from others with no intention of sharing.
2. Those who came to *learn* from others but found themselves sharing.
3. Those whose primary purpose in coming was to *share* with little thought of learning.
4. Those who came to *share* and *learn*, but found themselves controlled by the compulsion to impart their ideas to others without learning from them.
5. Those who came to do both—*share* and *learn*, but sadly were able to do neither.
6. Those who came to *share* and *learn* who thankfully did just that. Another example in life of a balance well maintained.

* * * *

Are You Sure This Is Mine?

XVII

*Do not be afraid, for I have redeemed you;
I have called you by your name, you are mine.
Should you pass through the sea, I will be
  with you;
or through rivers, they will not swallow you up.
Should you walk through fire, you will not
  be scorched
and the flames will not burn you.
For I am Yahweh, your God,
the Holy One of Israel, your savior.* (Isaiah 43:2-3)

AT FIRST, when I said, "God, I know you are there," it was enough to believe. I had perfect peace from acknowledging his existence, nothing more. I thought that peace would last forever. How I wish that it had. He let me rest in that security for a short time only. Soon I knew that I must read the Bible. I must study. I must learn and understand more about this God who called me back to him. The more I read, the more I understood, the more I knew that I would never understand. There was always more. Before long I knew that I did not pray enough.

Judy Gill Milford

I thought about God a lot, but I did not spend enough time talking with him, praising him. I also realized that I wasn't giving enough. How can I drift along content and happy when there is much that needs to be done? No matter how much I give and how much I do, it will never be enough.

* * * *

I hold on to pieces of myself. If I do as much as I should and give as much as I should give, won't I be filled with the spirit of God so that there will be nothing left of me? I am still too selfish to be willing to go that far. I still want to retain myself and the world. Can I take little steps? Can small steady continuous steps be better than giant hurdling jumps in which I stumble and fall back? or by holding back is it the worse kind of sin? Am I cutting myself off from God's grace? Can I be content with little bits of progress?

* * * *

I have sought God earnestly and I have fled from him. Maybe like St. Augustine who said, "Lord, make me chaste, but not yet," I want to be holy, but not yet. I seek God's face, but I always hold back. I am not ready to be scorned by the world. I am unable to seek *only* God.

* * * *

Are You Sure This Is Mine?

While we were on vacation this summer I read *As I Lay Dying* by William Faulkner. I have to confess that curiosity prompted me to read it. After it was banned in a nearby high school I wanted to know whether the objections were valid. It was a strange, sad book, but not nearly as objectionable as many I have seen.

* * * *

I have spent my entire life not wanting to die. The nights of lying awake trying to imagine the nothingness of not being—it never occurred to me to worry about aging. I don't think I ever expected to get that far. Well, the aging is accelerating and the feelings that evolve surprise me.

* * * *

My feelings about Grandpa Hollenback continue to be complicated even now, a year after his death.
   I tried to love him.
   Everyone is supposed to love Grandpa.
   I knew enough about his childhood
     to halfway understand
  his unsavory behavior and flaunted infidelities,
  but that was not enough to kindle love
    I thought that I should feel.
  I think I could have forgiven him

Judy Gill Milford

>   for the pain he caused throughout the years
>   if ever he had asked forgiveness
> but until his death, he never admitted wrong—
>   was never sorry.
> There was something about his dying
>   in that hospital room encircled
>   by our hands in prayer
>   that released me,
> But even now when I think of him
>   I feel cheated.

* * * *

My reluctance to forgive those who have not asked forgiveness is due, to some extent, to my pride—that dreadful pride once again. When forgiveness is sought it is much easier because we know that the offender has admitted to us that we are right and he was wrong.

* * * *

Every couple of days during free period, God looks down and says, "Judy is gaining. She is getting confidence and you know how she is. She will get puffed up with pride. We need to send a humbling experience." And he does.

* * * *

Are You Sure This Is Mine?

Sometimes, I think it would be nice to do something important, to get a spot in a history book or encyclopedia, to grab a little piece of immortality. It is human nature to do this either consciously or unconsciously. We go about it in different ways. Presidents, politicians, leaders of armies, movie stars, rock stars, great physicians, even contenders in *The Guinness Book of Records* have done something to assure that after they are gone there will be something to show that they were on this earth for a time.

One thing I have noticed, though, is that rarely do they take anyone with them. The most famous persons usually go into history alone, without the persons that they loved most beside them. So of what use is it? Would I want to make a name for myself only to leave my family of loved ones floating together without me in anonymity? That seems cold and lonely.

* * * *

St. Augustine said, "Never would such and so great things be by God wrought for us, if with the death of the body the life of the soul came to an end."[1]

When does the soul leave the body? Does it leave when the heart stops beating, or when the brain waves cease or when someone says "she's dead?" For that matter, when does the soul enter the body? At conception, at birth, at baptism?—couldn't be at

215

Judy Gill Milford

baptism because people have souls who never had baptism.

I don't think the soul dwells in a body with no heartbeat or brain waves. It just wouldn't be there—where no energy was, but when does it leave?

If soul enters at conception what happens to all those little souls who die before their time, the ones who are never free to make choices? Are they gathered back in to God unused? I don't think they are out there somewhere suffering separation, aloneness. They don't deserve that. Surely there is a special place for barely used souls.

* * * *

In *Seven Storey Mountain* Merton tells us that "Souls are like athletes, that need opponents worthy of them, if they are to be tried and extended and pushed to the full use of their powers, and rewarded according to their capacity."[2]

* * * *

Of all things God created, sometimes I think that he must love trees best. I know that they cannot think and they don't have a soul, but they can stand secure in their block of time, caress the earth and feel the seasons change. The wind ruffles their leaves and

Are You Sure This Is Mine?

rain showers cleanse them. They are strong, independent and loved. What could be better than that?

* * * *

As an aide I work mostly with three or four children at a time giving them special attention where needed to help them to catch up. Sometimes, I help by grading papers. I cannot forget a page of fill-in-blanks that I checked last week. One sentence read, "Is there gold at the end of the _____?" Instead of using *rainbow* Angela had filled in *manhole*. At first reading I laughed to myself as I marked it wrong. What an absurd sentence— "Is there gold at the end of the manhole?" Surely, everyone is familiar with the legend of finding a pot of gold at the end of a rainbow. Obviously, she had no idea what the sentence said.

Later, I realized that perhaps there is more truth to be found in this strange sentence than in the old legend. None of us really expects to find a pot of gold at the end of the rainbow, but finding God at the lowest point in our lives is much like finding gold at the bottom of the manhole.

* * * *

In reading "The Way of Life—an Examination of Conscience" in the March, 1989, issue of *The Word*

Judy Gill Milford

Among Us, I saw myself as I did not want to. This article tells us that "if we take our eyes off the Lord when we are examining our conscience, we may become self-centered and introspective." Who is more introspective than I am? Hardly anyone that I can think of. Commandment one tells us that we must have no other gods before the Lord our God. Do I make a god out of my work, my possessions—or my image in the eyes of others so that these rule my life instead of God? Of the ten commandments it looks as if I fail most miserably on number one. Surely that must be most important, since God put it first. Does that make me the most unholy?

* * * *

What am I supposed to do? This work that I have done since October is important. I hope I have helped some of the children but I'm using up so much of myself. How far must I go? I need to write. I need time to be alone with my thoughts. Is that selfish? Is there a middle line—a balance between the two? I feel some of my enthusiasm waning or should I say draining, although I still enjoy the children.

Another problem is the change in approach. When we changed the format after Christmas my relationship with the children became less natural. The rush to finish a lesson in a day or to read X number of pages takes away from the spontaneity which for me enabled the situation to thrive. Maybe I am kidding

Are You Sure This Is Mine?

myself. Maybe I was not helping that much before. Maybe they were never learning anything.

* * * *

This afternoon the entire school went to a play, *The Hunchback of Notre Dame*, based on the novel of that name by Victor Hugo. My first thoughts were that the children would not be interested. I was wrong. It was presented well and they were captivated. I do think the second-graders were somewhat lost when they got to the most important part. "How can I be anything more than what people believe me to be?" Quasimodo says. Where does truth lie? Is it within the man? I would say yes, but if in interacting with others, there are negative reactions, does that in itself become a part of the truth? If man is alone, totally to himself, he is what he is, but in society can he ever be just that? With others he is always partly what he appears to be, not just what he is. In the play we see the priest, who would be for the most the symbol for good, portrayed as evil itself. In his twisted mind he convinced himself that his evil deeds were justified. The girl-witch-gypsy was to the priest the embodiment of evil. He saw her as a temptation leading others into sin when in fact she was kind and gentle. And Quasimodo—the priest viewed him because of his affliction as one of the poor lost souls but we are allowed to view his goodness and purity. He and Esmeralda reach out to each other in

Judy Gill Milford

their wretchedness. In our exalted state we can do nothing. In our pain we can reach out to others. Healing can take place.

* * * *

Somewhere between the concept of an individual that exists within his own mind and the illusion of the individual that is viewed by outsiders, lies the reality that is the man. Each holds an element of truth inaccessible to the other. But more than that, the man is constantly changing and the observer's view of him is ever-changing. Perhaps the only adequate reality of a man can be found in God's perception of that man—a reality that humans cannot know, a reality that transcends time and encompasses all that a person is, was and will be.

* * * *

On spring break this year Will and I went with my niece and nephew, and my mom and dad back to my mom's childhood home, Scranton, Pennsylvania. Later, we went to Cedar Grove to visit Smokey's wife. I gave her a copy of the poem I wrote about him. In visiting her that evening I realized something. Smokey died before his daughter was old enough to remember him. For forty-two years I have carried memories of his kindness to me when I was a little girl. For forty-two years I have thought of him

Are You Sure This Is Mine?

as my friend, as a man who understood children and cared about me. Now, I realize that by all rights my memories of him belong to her, Karen, his daughter, the little girl who never got the chance to know her dad. That is so unfair. Why does that happen?

* * * *

Everywhere we strive for self-gratification. So many books and articles aimed at promoting the self of the individual. Women are encouraged to put themselves before their husbands and their children. Husbands do the same. Isn't it impossible to nurture and support Christianity in a "me-first" society. What is happening to the world?

* * * *

It has been twelve years now since Marilyn died. I still think about Chuck and Page, the children she left behind. They lost her when they were too young to remember all their good times. But I remember . . . so many things. The tuna salad we ate on fritos. Her love of Steve McQueen and Steve Lawrence. The way she called me Gilhooley and laughed at my feet but lent me her best angora sweater for a special date. The way she told everyone my first words to her were "Hi, I'm Judy and I'm left-handed." The Lettermen concert. The glow she had when she first told me of her love for Charlie, their dad. I think of

Judy Gill Milford

her when I look at blue-eyed Chris. She always told me that someday I would marry a blue-eyed boy and ruin his chances of having blue-eyed children (Chris is the only one). I wish there were some way that I could give her children a gift of all those wonderful memories I have of her. She lives for me in those memories.

* * * *

Are You Sure This Is Mine?

XVIII

Out of his infinite glory, may he give you the power through his Spirit for your hidden self to grow strong, so that Christ may live in your hearts through faith, and then, planted in love and built on love, you will with all the saints have strength to grasp the breadth and the length, the height and the depth; until, knowing the love of Christ, which is beyond all knowledge, you are filled with the utter fullness of God. (Ephesians 3:16-19)

EACH morning I wake up on empty. I ask Jesus to fill me with love—for him. Maybe I have to write up all this emptiness before I can be filled. Maybe I have to set aside my writing before I can be filled—I don't know.

I do know that I have to put God first. I have to seek him first and sometimes, most times I want something else more. Is that the reason for the emptiness?

* * * *

Judy Gill Milford

What is the answer to the abortion issue? The world is overcrowded. Resources are being used too quickly. One simple, partial solution is to side with pro-choicers who favor abortion. Why not? Abortion gets rid of a few million, doesn't it?

Pro-choicers are quick to tell us that if abortion is banned, illegal abortions will rise—illegal abortions which will jeopardize the health and safety of millions of women. I cannot dispute this speculation. Does this fact make it moral to kill unborn babies? I don't think so.

And, why do some anti-abortion demonstrators use force? Don't they realize that type of action does nothing for their credibility?

* * * *

Where is the pride of Americans? I remember watching the patriotic war movies of the forties, standing misty-eyed through "The Star-Spangled Banner," or with my chest stuck out and hand over heart for the pledge. I don't see that pride being encouraged in our schools today or anyplace else. What has happened to American patriotism? Have we been subjected to too much truth? And if that is the problem, what are we doing about it?

* * * *

Are You Sure This Is Mine?

In some ways I don't like the person I am becoming since I started writing. I know that I must carefully maintain the balance of my life. To lose oneself in God for love of others is acceptable, even desirable, but to lose oneself in writing is to lose one's self in self. That is dangerous.

* * * *

Oh Jesus, I have unknowingly pushed you to the back of my life afraid that if I spend too much time with you now there will be no time to grasp each moment. Knowing that I must not choose the world in your place I tried to convince myself that writing was so necessary to the fulfillment of your plan for my life that it was all right to put it first—you last. I am suffering the consequences of that unconscious choice.

* * * *

One of the children got up early to find me on the living room sofa. She asked if Rob and I had a fight. She doesn't have to worry about that. I got up to write down thoughts that were exploding in the dark with no place to go. Through twenty-three years of marriage Rob and I have followed my mom's sage advice, "Never go to bed mad at each other." I don't believe we ever have. It is a good thing not to leave

Judy Gill Milford

loose stones lying around when you go to bed. In a few days, or weeks, or months, you may find a wall has been erected and you may not even know where it came from.

* * * *

How much pain can a person know and still be able to appreciate joy—is there a measured amount which renders beauty useless, life futile?

We have the power to choose some of what we store. To absorb all corruption, evil, pain that we find in the world serves no good purpose. We must absorb some to realize that changes need to be made but to store all would leave a person hopeless. I must have hope to exist and to be useful. What happens to the man who by choice or through no fault of his has stored too much pain? Does he turn to food, drugs, alcohol, suicide or perhaps a new world created by himself?

And, wouldn't some people have a higher tolerance for this pain just as there is difference in tolerance for actual physical pain? Would not some people also have a better filtering system or ability to choose what to store?

* * * *

Our daughter is having a problem with love. I am amazed at the extent to which her problem becomes

Are You Sure This Is Mine?

my own. How do you deal with a pain that is not your own but is so real that it threatens your very being? That pain is one that I gladly bear if it could help her bear her own, but such a helpless pain for I am powerless to be relieved unless or until she can deal with hers.

I can see a correlation between this willingness to suffer for a loved one and the willingness of Jesus to die for us. Oh, I don't mean that I presume to be Christlike in my concern for my daughter—not at all. It is just that this situation helps me to understand Christ's willingness, or the magnitude of his love and sacrifice.

* * * *

In a recent movie, *Accidental Tourist,* Macon tells Sarah, "maybe it's not how much you love someone that counts, but who you are when you are with them." That statement made me think of a poem by Roy Croft called "Love" that I wish I had written which begins

> I love you,
> Not only for what you are,
> But for what I am
> When I am with you.

Another stanza continues:

> I love you
> For putting your hand

Judy Gill Milford

> Into my heaped-up heart
> And passing over
> All the foolish, weak things
> That you can't help
> Dimly seeing there,
> And for drawing out
> Into the light
> All the beautiful belongings
> That no one else had looked
> Quite far enough to find.[1]

I am thankful for the person I love. Thankful for who I am when I am with him. For years I have known that somehow with him I am the best that I can be. I never have to strain to seem more than I am, never have to put on a false face. I am always free to be. I want that for my children—that each one of them will find someone who will encourage growth.

* * * *

Rob and I are different. He is content to accept. I search for answers. I know, without doubt, if I had been Eve and he Adam, I would have tempted him. I would have been the one to taste the Tree of Knowledge seeking more, more, more. He has such natural goodness in him. To him right is right, wrong is wrong, and God is God. I ask, seek, search, probe. Heaven for me will be finding the *Complete Un-*

Are You Sure This Is Mine?

abridged Book of Answers to Life and knowing it is the correct edition.

* * * *

It slipped out easily and unintentionally before I knew what I was doing. Why didn't I bite my tongue, chew on the side of my mouth, anything to keep those dreadful words from tumbling forth? A parent doesn't say those words to gloat. Anything but that. At the moment we say them we are afraid that the child (or young adult) will not make the connection between our annoying warning and the actual outcome. If the connection is not made, the child will not learn from mistakes, causing more pain. Wouldn't we do just about anything to save our children? So we continue to say what we know we should not—"I told you so."

* * * *

Rob told me once (laughingly of course) that I would be better off if I didn't tell all of my mistakes. I cannot stand to make a mistake. I should be used to it. I've made enough of them. The only thing worse than the mistake is not being the first one to discover it. I find it painful when someone points out one of my errors that I have not already taken credit for. And what am I doing? Writing all my mistakes,

Judy Gill Milford

weaknesses and shortcomings for all to see. Writers must possess a special form of insanity to be willing to expose themselves this way.

* * * *

What is it about us that makes it important to get approval from others? I surprise and disappoint myself when in the company of friends I find myself reporting on some accomplishment of one of our children. I sit there with no intention of mentioning a test score, soccer play or some other minor example of brilliance, and before I know it the words tumble out with an eagerness that amazes me. And then to prove that I realize that these same children are not actually perfect, that I am able to view them objectively, I must relate some amusing anecdote revealing one of their not-too-serious flaws. Our children become an affirmation of self. If our children are alright, so are we. If they are not, either we feel that we have failed or we disassociate ourselves from them. Unintentionally, we come to live through them.

* * * *

Of all the time in history that I could have lived, I am alive now and I realize that my *now* is running out. Why do I find that so difficult to accept?

* * * *

Are You Sure This Is Mine?

With the onset of every spring and fall an indescribable feeling wells within and overflows—as if there is a stirring within me of every season change from the beginning of time. Is it possible that some people are born with a memory of past encounters with the earth? a memory that comes through the genes? I don't mean reincarnation, although I can see why some people find the idea desirable. To imagine reincarnation is much more acceptable than ceasing to exist altogether. That is oppressive.

Sometimes, when I think about dying my mind goes round and round in circles until I begin to lose momentum and slowly circle into a hole—like a steel ball circling the rim of a funnel-like apparatus until eventually the ball falls through and passes on.

* * * *

Reading Madeleine L'Engle's *Walking on Water* for the second time, I noticed something that I missed the first time. She said that some atheists deny the existence of God because they see the world around them as inconsistent with the loving caring God that they might conceive of. Perhaps that is the reason for some of my faith problems—those inconsistencies, for they certainly exist. But she is correct when she says that God must allow them if we are to have choice. Much of the pain and suffering in the world results from poor choices, selfish choices.

* * * *

Judy Gill Milford

I wish that Madeleine L'Engle lived right down the road from me—someone I could pick up the phone and talk to. Reading her books are like a visit with my best friend.

* * * *

To guard against madness I spend a carefully measured portion of each day predictably engaged. If I write too much or study too much or think too much, I may become so centered on one thing that I lose contact with the real world. I must carefully guard the balance lest the scales be tipped.

* * * *

My soul is a man
thirsting in the desert
wary of the wiles of mirage
that ageless trickster,
Yet seeking desperately seeking
Life-sustaining water.
Like Moses disobedient
I wander in search of Canaan.
What must I do to find
The Promised Land—
The Promised One?

* * * *

Are You Sure This Is Mine?

Will's friends in the neighborhood found a bird in the yard with a smashed wing. I put some worms by its beak, but it was too weak to eat. Insects were already busy at work in the wound. Why would they begin decomposing it before the life had slipped away? A terrible death.

* * * *

I am taking myself someplace I have never been and it is a little frightening. For years I have kept myself so carefully in check. "Oh no, I couldn't possibly handle that job." "There are many others who could do a better job." "I'm not qualified for that."

Since I started writing I know who I am. I know what I can do—what I have been preparing to do my entire life. That knowledge gives me a confidence I have never known. In some ways it is very satisfying, exciting, exhilarating. On the other hand, there are aspects of the life I have always had that are so good—so right, that I know I must do nothing to jeopardize their continuance. No matter how involved I become in writing and my study to improve, I must sustain the balance. Rob and the children are the most important.

* * * *

Judy Gill Milford

Oh God, I acknowledge to you that I have sinned against you. I have taken the first commandment and given it tenth position. Without realizing it I have let other gods creep into my life and their positions have become exalted.

And just now, for a moment, I, like Eve, was not going to accept responsibility for my sin. I was going to say, "The devil made me do it." A small voice inside me said, "Judy, you can taste the fruit. You can have perfect knowledge. You don't need God. You are a big, strong, intelligent person. You can do it yourself."

I stand before you now and admit that I am nothing without you. I need your strength. I need your holiness. Without you I have no strength, no holiness. I am a single person working toward a single purpose. If that purpose is not yours, the strength is not there.

Help me to be ever mindful that I must rely on you daily for guidance, that I must keep you in focus, that I must never take my eyes from you. When I do, I lose direction, purpose and strength.

* * * *

Once I went directly from not knowing if there was a God, and considering him merely the symbol for good with Satan the symbol for evil, to being so grateful to him, abiding in him, resting in his care. There was no time when I thought about the possibil-

Are You Sure This Is Mine?

ity of being "saved" or "not saved"—the possibility of going to hell because I had chosen worldliness over Godliness. For the first time I know what it feels like to wonder about going to the "other place." I know I don't want to spend eternity alone. I have learned on earth that when I retreat into myself and depend on my self only the loneliness is more than I can bear. I must reach out to God. Knowing this I must continue to persevere throughout to the end of my life always searching, always seeking to know God and to provide an adequate dwelling place for the Holy Spirit within me.

* * * *

We have reached a new stage of our life. The children of our friends have begun to marry in increasing numbers. Last year there was one wedding, this summer five. After the wedding last weekend, guests released helium balloons outside the church for the joyous occasion. I started thinking. The same thing could be done for funerals, couldn't it? Mourners could write a special message of love or tribute to the deceased for each balloon. Or if the person was to be cremated, some of his ashes could be put in each balloon. What a send-off. I'm not so sure I would want to be cremated, but I rather like the idea of landing in a tree, on a cardinal's wing, a daffodil, a waterfall, or in a mountain stream. . . .

* * * *

Judy Gill Milford

After Robbie's soccer game tonight we were having the usual conversation where he explains to me all the ref's calls from the game that I didn't understand. I made a light remark about a call that had been made against him. That kind of remark usually inspires a snappy humorous come-back from him. Tonight, he blew up and ended by saying that after games we criticize but never tell him he played a good game. I couldn't believe what I was hearing. Aren't I the foolish mother sitting in the bleachers with her eyes glued on "00" the entire game, the one who silently seethes when other fans yell at her son, the same mother who goes to every possible game as a spell against his possible injury? So many misunderstandings occur from a failure to communicate.

* * * *

Many times when I am writing a poem, I am so charged with emotion that I think I say some things that I do not. Some of what I am feeling or thinking does not come through, but I do not even know it because I am so close to it.

* * * *

The same thing happens when we are raising our children. Thoughts and feelings that we take for granted are not clear to them, resulting in misunderstanding. We love them so much that we don't think

Are You Sure This Is Mine?

it is necessary to say anything. Sometimes they need to hear that we love and are proud of them. As the villain in *Cool Hand Luke* was fond of saying, "What we have here is a failure to communicate." I wonder how many times I have failed all my children just as I failed Robbie the other night because of a "failure to communicate?"

* * * *

John had cataract surgery today. Physically he came through fine, but mentally not so good. He worried so much about a claustrophobic reaction to the confinement of the surgery that he was in an agitated state from the beginning. Now, he is unable to stay in one place for five minutes. We cannot figure out what to do to help him.

* * * *

John went back to the doctor this morning. At first he thought he was helped by getting the patch off his eye, but he is still not well. He is going to see his internist tomorrow. Maybe something is out of balance physically in his body that can be adjusted.

* * * *

We went from doctor to doctor today but did not find out anything to help him. He was a lot like this

Judy Gill Milford

the year we took him to Hilton Head. Usually John is so reasonable. I got the feeling today that our words of encouragement just make him mad—almost like he is determined to feel bad and doesn't want anyone to interfere with his misery. I'm trying to understand why someone would focus on negative feelings. I am at a loss.

* * * *

In a way I feel guilty because I think about the time I am losing when I need to be writing. I know that he is most important and all my energy needs to be spent helping him. If I cannot support him and help him to feel better, my purpose in writing is meaningless.

* * * *

I try to imagine how it must feel to be almost seventy-eight and know that most of your life has been lived. I begin to see some of what he must be going through. Is he pushing us away in an attempt to make the inevitable parting easier? Is there something deep within him that tells him if he worries enough and focuses on every possible problem eventually he will be glad that it is all over? He almost said that yesterday. He said that he felt so bad that it would be a relief not to have to go on. He does not enjoy the grandchildren any more.

Are You Sure This Is Mine?

How can I convince him that it will be easier for us all if we hold each other close for now. If we nourish our love, he can take some of us, some of his grandchildren, with him when he goes, and we can keep a lot of him with us. I want to remember the fun times —like the animated narration of the horse he raced in India during World War II or the long talks he and I had about religion in my living room. I don't want to remember the way he snapped at me yesterday when I tried to encourage. That is not the John I know—the one I want the children to remember.

* * * *

And doesn't he know that he could outlive me? He could have twenty years of living ahead of him and they will be such lonely painful years if he doesn't find some joy.

* * * *

God, help me to find some answers for John. He doesn't want to be like this. He remembers his own dad at ninety and he remembers Fonnie and that is not what he wants. Please help us to help him to find a path back to the living until you are ready for him to come to you. He does not deserve the place in between where he is now—the living hell. Help him to find joy in you.

* * * *

Judy Gill Milford

Father in heaven, I do not like myself much right now. Usually, it is a pleasure to give my time to others—to help them any way that I can. Right now I need my time. I want to finish a book and John needs me. Why did this problem come now when I am selfish about my time? Is it possible that I was never meant to finish this book? Have I taken on something that is beyond my ability?

I know that I must place my trust in you. If my writing does not glorify you, if it does not help others, if it does not help me to focus on you and love you more, it has no purpose.

* * * *

The terrible shrinking that I observed in my dad in ICU after his surgery two years ago has taken place in John. Suddenly he is living in a world of one. The world is revolving around him spinning out of control. Dad's world reopened, so John's surely can too.

* * * *

Why is everything so hard for me or rather, why do I make things hard for myself? I read, study and learn, but I do not really know truth until I experience it myself.

* * * *

Are You Sure This Is Mine?

While on earth, are we off-shoots or sparks from the spirit of God? Heaven then would be gathering of all worthy souls to the entity of God. God continues to prevail over evil. He maintains ultimate strength over the devil. Those who love God live in a selfless love. At their death they are rejoined or made one with God because all who truly love God are united and are one.

Satan will never prevail because those spirits who succumb to his temptation are consumed by selfish or worldly endeavors, therefore they are never working for others. Instead of bonding with or becoming one with Satan as the holy ones are joined to God, self-serving spirits continue alone. Thus Satan's strength is never replenished in the same way as God's.

* * * *

One of the best things about being is just that—being. Being inside myself, looking, seeing, observing, experiencing, enjoying, but most of all thinking. Recently, I realized that one of the things that I dread most about dying is the possibility or probability of being separated from my thoughts. I thought that perhaps hell would be separation from self. For a while that made sense.

In reading *The Eternal Now* several years ago I noted that Paul Tillich defined loneliness as the "pain of being alone" and solitude as the "glory of

Judy Gill Milford

being alone." I do not know loneliness but long for solitude. Is this then what my "hell" would be? To cling so ferociously to my precious "self" only to find that being alone with my self in eternity would constitute not "solitude" but "loneliness" because I would have given up all love, all others for this, would be the ultimate irony. Separation from God to be with self exclusively would leave only the "pain of being alone."

* * * *

Yahweh has been angry with me on your account; he has sworn that I shall not cross the Jordan or enter the prosperous land which Yahweh your God is giving you as your heritage. Yes, I am to die in this country; I shall not go across this Jordan; you will go over and take possession of that rich land. Take care therefore not to forget the convenant which Yahweh your God has made with you by making a carved image of anything that Yahweh your God has forbidden you; for Yahweh your God is a consuming fire, a jealous God. (Deut. 21-24)

* * * *

I know that I have sinned. I have felt God's anger, his face turned from me, but I need not fear that he will keep me from the promised land. We are under a new law. That is what the salvation of Jesus Christ

Are You Sure This Is Mine?

is all about! He has taken those sins on himself. Therefore, I do not have to continue to carry the self-destructive guilt of those sins—the sin of doubt, of putting other gods before the one Holy God.

References

Except as otherwise noted, all scripture citations are from *The Jerusalem Bible* (Garden City: Doubleday & Company, Inc. 1968).

Chapter 1

1. *The Holy Bible*, King James Version. Philadelphia: National Bible Press.
2. Roy Palmer, *Cokesbury Hymnal*, p. 122.

Chapter 3

1. Gene Stratton-Porter, *The Keeper of the Bees*. New York: Doubleday, Page & Company. 1925. p. 514.

Chapter 4

1. F. J. Sheed, *Christ in Eclipse,* Kansas City: Sheed Andrews and McMeel, Inc. 1978.

Chapter 9

1. *Good News New Testament.* New York: American Bible Study. 1977.

Judy Gill Milford

Chapter 10

1. Thomas a Kempis, *Imitation of Christ*. Garden City: Image Books. 1955.
2. Thomas H. Green, S. J., *When the Well Runs Dry*. Notre Dame, Indiana: Ave Maria Press. 1985.

Chapter 11

1. Thomas Merton, *The Seven Storey Mountain*. New York: Harcourt, Brace and Company, Inc. 1961.

Chapter 15

1. Philip St. Romain, "Journey to the Center of Your Soul," *Liguorian*, Volume 76, September, 1988, p. 10.
2. Ibid. p. 12.
3. Malcolm Muggeridge, *A Third Testament*. Canada: Little, Brown & Company. 1976.
4. Ibid.
5. Michael Mott, *The Seven Mountains of Thomas Merton*. Boston: Houghton Mifflin Company. 1984.
6. Thomas Merton, *Love and Living*. New York: Farrar, Straus & Giroux, Inc. 1979.

Chapter 17

1. Saint Augustine, *Confessions*, translated by R. S. Pine-Coffin. England: Penguin Classics. 1961.
2. Thomas Merton, *Seven Storey Mountain*.

Are You Sure This Is Mine?

Chapter 18

1. Ray Croft, "Love," *The Best Loved Poems of the American People*. Garden City: Garden City Publishing Co. 1936.

248.48/MIL

1304020
Are you sure this is mine : a searc...
Milford, Judy Gill.

JAN. 0
FEB 02 1991
Feb. 16, '92

282.081
MIL   Milford, Judy
             Are you sure this is mine?